Confronting the
SCHOOL
DROPOUT
CRISIS

I dedicate this book to my three daughters, April, Melissa, and Autumn. You were my inspiration to continue my education. You were my cheerleaders and helpers even in the midst of surviving a life full of uncertainty and poverty.

I also dedicate this book to anyone who is attempting to reach and encourage young people who are at risk of dropping out of school. Don't ever stop believing in them and their potential.

Confronting the

SCHOOL DROPOUT CRISIS

Insights and Interventions From a Former Dropout

SUSAN BOWMAN

Foreword by Jim Rex

CORWIN

For information:

Corwin
A Sage Company
2455 Teller Road
Thousand Oaks, California 91320
(800) 233-9936
www.corwin.com

Sage Publications Ltd.
1 Oliver's Yard
55 City Road
London EC1Y 1SP
United Kingdom

Sage Publications India Pvt. Ltd.
Unit No 323-333, Third Floor, F-Block
International Trade Tower Nehru Place
New Delhi 110 019
India

Sage Publications Asia-Pacific Pte. Ltd.
18 Cross Street #10-10/11/12
China Square Central
Singapore 048423

Vice President and Editorial Director:
  Monica Eckman
Publisher: Jessica Allan
Content Development Editor:
  Mia Rodriguez
Content Development Manager:
  Lucas Schleicher
Senior Editorial Assistant:
  Natalie Delpino
Production Editor: Vijayakumar
Copy Editor: Diane DiMura
Typesetter: TNQ Tech Pvt. Ltd.
Proofreader: Girish Sharma
Indexer: TNQ Tech Pvt. Ltd.
Cover Designer: Gail Buschman
Marketing Manager: Olivia Bartlett

Printed in the United States of America

Paperback ISBN 978-1-0719-6214-5

This book is printed on acid-free paper.

25 26 27 28 29 10 9 8 7 6 5 4 3 2 1

Contents

Acknowledgments   ix

About the Author   xi

Foreword by Jim Rex   xiii

Chapter 1. Why This Book?   1

Chapter 2. The High Cost of Dropping Out   5

The Impact of Dropping Out   7

Chapter 3. The Reasons Students Drop Out   11

Academic Challenges   11

Disconnection and Disengagement   11

Chronic Discipline Problems   12

Lack of School Resources and Supports   12

Technology and Social Media Interference   13

History of Chronic Absenteeism and Truancy   14

Bullying and School Violence   14

Family Mental and/or Physical Health Issues   15

Peer Influence   15

Substance Abuse Issues   16

Language, Racial, and Cultural Disparity   16

Extreme Poverty   17

Pregnancy   17

Lack of Grit and Fostering Resiliency and a
    Self-Encouraging Mindset   18

Desire for More Personal Freedom   19

Chapter 4. What We Can Learn From Students   21

What We Can Learn From Students Who Almost Dropped Out   21

Insights From Students After They Dropped Out   28

Personal Stories From School Dropouts   29

Chapter 5. Strategies to Reach Students at Risk of Dropping Out   41

Addressing Students' Mental Health Needs   41

Reaching Students Who Avoid Seeking Out Help From Others   43

Helping Students Find and Create Connection   48

Providing Restorative Discipline Practices   50

Developing and Enhancing a Personal Support System   52

Small Support and Counseling Groups   53

Student Peer Helping and Mentoring   56

Home Visits   59

Encouraging Personal Strengths and Purpose   61

Starting Early Is Best   64

Remembering It's Never Too Late   66

Peer Support   67

Chapter 6. Nine Strategies to Strengthen Dropout Prevention   73

Chapter 7. Increasing Parent/Guardian Involvement   77

Chapter 8. Advice From Former Dropouts   81

Nina   81

Jose   81

Larissa   82

Travis   82

Anita   83

James   83

Appendix A Screening Tool to Identify Students at
    Higher Risk for Dropping Out   89

Appendix B Suggested Programs and Initiatives to Help
    Students Stay in School   91

Appendix C Famous People Who Faced Challenges
    But Never Gave Up   95

Appendix D Quotes to Encourage Students at Risk for
    Dropping Out   99

Appendix E "The Old Leather Jacket"   103

References   109

Index   115

Visit the companion website at
www.schoolsweneednow.com
for downloadable resources.

Acknowledgments

I want to thank Acceleration Academies, Excel Academy, Essential Education, and Jean Riley of Synergy School for allowing me to use several success stories of students who attended your programs. I am very encouraged that programs like yours exist to provide a second chance to potential school dropouts. Thank you, Dr. Ed Orszulak, director of Futures School, for all your years of dedication to helping students with challenging behaviors and developmental disabilities to stay in school.

I want to especially acknowledge my husband, Dr. Bob Bowman, for all his help with this book. We make a great team and have always been each other's editor and sounding board of ideas. Thanks for all your advice and how each time I had you review it, you would tell me it needed more! Your support and guidance have been extremely helpful in writing something that I hope can be impactful and useful to anyone who works with young people. Thanks for all your understanding and encouragement!

I also thank God for making this book possible by always providing and guiding me throughout the years. Without Him I would not be where I am today.

> With man this is impossible, but with God all things are possible.
>
> Matthew 19:26

PUBLISHER'S ACKNOWLEDGMENT

Corwin gratefully acknowledges the contributions of the following reviewer:
Leslie Goines
School Counselor
Metropolis, Illinois

About the Author

Susan Bowman has an Education Specialist (EdS) degree in Counselor Education from the University of South Carolina. She worked as a secondary school counselor, a licensed professional counselor, and social worker specializing in helping troubled teens and their families. She also worked as a Title I counselor for the South Carolina Department of Juvenile Justice and started a nonprofit organization to help incarcerated youth. She has conducted seminars throughout the United States and abroad for educators on creative strategies for working with troubled adolescents. In 2005, the GED Testing Service awarded Susan with its highest honor, the Cornelius P. Turner Award, named for the founder of the GED Testing Program. This award is presented annually to a GED graduate who has made outstanding contributions to society in education, justice, health, public service, and social welfare. Susan was cofounder of Developmental Resources, an educational consulting company that provided national and international seminars and conferences. She was also cofounder of YouthLight, Inc., an educational publishing company.

Susan is currently coowner of YouthHope Consulting, LLC and consults and publishes books on how to work with troubled children and adolescents. She has been interviewed by the *Arizona Tribune* and the *Wall Street Journal* and numerous radio stations across the country. Her book on self-injury was recognized in *USA Today*.

She has authored and coauthored more than twenty books and programs. Her memoir, *Breaking Free: A Teenage Runaway's Story of Survival and Triumph*, is about her personal journey, which started when she dropped out of eighth grade and ran away from home. By age nineteen, after having her third child, she finally broke free of the toxic relationship with her daughters' father and had to depend on welfare as her only means of financial support. She struggled as a teen mom to complete her education and make a better life for her and her daughters. With the help of a mentor, she received her GED and then went on to pursue several college degrees.

Susan can be reached at sbowman@youthlightbooks.com.

Foreword

///

During my service as South Carolina's 16th State Superintendent of Education (2007–11), there was no problem more vexing or heartbreaking than the state's dropout rate. The human and societal toll was significant. Today, across much of America, human potential and achievement continue to be limited when our youth miss out on the benefits of remaining in school and completing their secondary education.

During my career, I have listened to and read the advice and research offered by many experts as to what should be done to reduce our nation's dropout rates. Many experts had worthwhile strategies, statistics, and in some cases programs. However, many lacked the ability to fully empathize with and therefore effectively describe the emotional, social, and educational realities that our dropouts experience during their critical and often traumatic school years. This lack of empathy and personal insight on the part of many experts was not as a result of their lack of concern or compassion for the plight of kids who drop out. No, the real reason was the majority of experts on the causes that end school success were never themselves so unsuccessful in school that they, themselves, dropped out of school. Most were successful academic achievers in school—not school "failures." School dropouts, let alone runaways, don't write books on the causes of, and remedies for, our dropout crisis—until now!

Susan Bowman, the author of this compelling book, is not only a former dropout and runaway herself, but her struggles from her preteen years to her eventual triumphs as a young adult are inspirational. Her expertise as an educator and counselor who has worked with thousands of at-risk youth is augmented by her lived experiences as a distraught and alienated preteen, teenager, and single teenage mother of three.

Throughout this book, the author masterfully intertwines her personal story, creative and illustrative vignettes, and an array of strategies and resources to provide a comprehensive set of insights and interventions that are powerful, introspective, and researched based. Susan has managed to exhibit an empathy in this book with the young dropout—through her personal story—that is lacking in so many other attempts to address this issue. Certainly, her training, expertise, and clinical experience are important to the successful impact of this book, but her recognizable and earned empathy with dropouts and their struggles—through her own survival stories—distinguishes this book from others on this subject.

If you want a comprehensive and enjoyable reading experience on the prevention of, and, when necessary, remediation of the consequences of school dropouts, I highly recommend *Confronting the School Dropout Crisis* by Susan Bowman—an empathetic survivor.

Jim Rex, PhD

Why This Book?

//

Children dropping out of school has been an ongoing problem for decades. Approximately 7,000 students in the United States drop out of high school every day (Barrington, 2023; Serani, 2020). When a student drops out, it impacts the school, community, nation, and especially the student and their family. Knowing this, school personnel have implemented many different initiatives to reduce the dropout rates in their schools. Unfortunately, the dropout rates continue to be far too high. According to the National Center for Education Statistics (NCES; 2024), "in 2022, there were 2.1 million status dropouts between the ages of 16 and 24." This increase was partially because of the effect the pandemic had on education, but it would be unfair to blame the current crisis entirely on COVID-19. This book was written to provide a wake-up call to professional educators to think about why the dropout crisis is continuing and provide more impactful interventions to address it.

I have read many books about school dropouts written by current and former educators who had a wealth of experience working with students. These educators offered insightful advice to teachers, counselors, and other school personnel. I admire these and others who have invested many years in the field of education and have so much experience to share with educators who are struggling with how to help a new generation of students stay in school. I have noticed, however, that almost all the authors who have written about dropout prevention and truancy initiatives have not actually experienced what it is like to struggle to stay in school and the challenges that follow. This book has been heavily influenced by my own personal experience as a former school dropout. I have included several stories about the challenges I faced and eventually overcame and added helpful insights and suggestions. In addition, I include stories and learnings from other school dropouts. My personal story of dropping out is intertwined throughout the book. In the last chapter, I provide readers with the rest of my story.

I have included stories and insights about the early warning signs of dropping out, which often start in elementary school. This information can be helpful in identifying ways school personnel can take action in helping to prevent young students from dropping out in the future. I also wanted to share some of the knowledge I gained while working as a middle school dropout prevention counselor, as a Title I counselor for incarcerated youth, and as a high school counselor.

I deeply believe we need to revisit how schools are addressing the problem of dropping out and incorporate fresh interventions that can reach all students. It is important for our young people to believe that regardless of who they are, where they come from, or what they have done, they are welcome in our schools, we believe in them and their potential, and we have their backs!

Even with decades of research and many actionable attempts to address the dropout crisis, this issue continues to be a chronic problem. We owe it to our children to do more to help them survive in school and thrive in our society by providing improved opportunities to access advanced education, better employment, and subsequently, quality of life. We gain many benefits from investing more wisely in our young people's educational experiences. Such initiatives have the potential to save our country up to $200 billion per year over the course of these young peoples' lifetimes (Hale & Canter, 2023).

This book is written primarily for those who work directly with students at high risk, such as school counselors, social workers, mental health professionals, nurses, school administrators, behavioral specialists, dropout prevention personnel, ISS (in-school suspension) facilitators, and any others who work directly with students. Classroom teachers can also gain some insights and strategies from this book to help them better understand and make connections with these students. I hope this book provides you with some unique perspectives that will help you have a more substantial impact on these students.

My Personal Story

Since I was in third grade, I felt a noticeable disconnection with school. I struggled with a learning disability throughout my elementary years and never felt that I belonged. By the time I entered fifth grade, I started to avoid going to school. It didn't help that my family had experienced several traumatic events while I was still in elementary school: When I was 12 years old my father was diagnosed with schizophrenia and was committed to a state mental hospital. I also had an older sister who almost died when she was 15 years old from a self-inflicted gunshot wound. Today, these would be labeled as adverse childhood experiences (ACEs), which we now have learned can contribute to chronic absenteeism and may eventually lead to dropping out.

I would try anything to stay home and avoid school. Pretending to be sick occasionally worked, but after several times the school nurse insisted my parents take me for a physical checkup. The doctor determined that nothing was physically wrong with me to keep me from going to school. Chronic absenteeism was not as common in the late 1960s. My small elementary school in the northeast of the United States lacked the knowledge of how to deal with a student who was chronically skipping school. We did not have a counselor in our school or anyone else who I felt I could really talk to. So, when pretending to be sick stopped working, I just acted like I was going to school and hid out in my yard or in our carport outside. In fifth grade I missed so many days of school I was told I needed to repeat the grade, which just added to my discouragement. I somehow survived and made it through elementary school, and the next year I started the seventh grade at the only middle school in our small town.

By the time I was 13, I started to become involved in more risky and defiant behavior. I began smoking cigarettes and marijuana and started drinking alcohol. I became more interested in boys but was a late bloomer and felt boys were not attracted to me. My friends and I would hang out on the weekends at a "drop-in" center that was for teens. How ironic that name was, when many who went there ended up "dropping out." Kids my age would meet and hang out there, but under adult supervision. I met a guy there who would change my entire life! Kevin was five years older than I and had dropped out of school. He wore bell-bottom jeans and had an earring and long, blond hair. He was different—and just the kind of guy who attracted me. Of course, I was also excited to have an older guy attracted to me. He seemed very caring at first, but over time he pressured me into having sex with him. After this happened, I felt like I now "belonged" to him instead of being in an amicable girlfriend/boyfriend relationship. My parents tried their best to keep me from seeing him, but I would sneak out of our house late at night. Kevin encouraged me to skip school; I would arrive at the

(Continued)

(Continued)

front entrance of the school and just walk out a back or side door, where I would meet up with him and we would go to the woods across the street. After skipping school on a regular basis, he eventually convinced me to leave my family and run away with him so we could live without my parents interfering in our relationship. It sounded like a great escape into a new world of adventure. Little did I know that I was now entrusting myself into the hands of an emotionally troubled person who had already impregnated another girl my age.

During this time, I felt like I had slipped into a deep, dark hole and I did not see a ladder to help me climb out. I had set off on an unforeseen journey over which I had no control. Fortunately, through intensive and continual effort and support from several sources, I was able to eventually turn my life around. My journey took me from dropping out of eighth grade and running away from home, to eventually obtaining a graduate degree and becoming a licensed therapist, author, and international presenter. More about this part of my story can be found later in the book.

I have gained many insights about the real world experienced by many school dropouts. Because of this, I remain highly motivated to researching, collecting, and pulling together information to help educators better understand and prevent students from dropping out and to intervene with teens who have already dropped out. *We can do better!*

When students feel disconnected and discouraged, they become vulnerable to making choices that can be destructive in the short and long term. Without having a personal connection to at least one encouraging adult in the school, these students often become easy targets for negative peer influence and/or dangerous relationships with others. These choices eventually result in new difficulties that accumulate and can lead to even more uncertainty, including emotional and physical hardship. Or they can cause a student to turn inward and engage in self-harming behaviors. The key is early detection and preventive interventions so these emotional and physical hardships can be avoided.

The High Cost of Dropping Out

///

In 1961, the National Education Association began the Project on School Dropouts. Daniel Schreiber, a school principal in New York, initiated the program to help more than 50,000 disadvantaged children. He firmly believed that "the United States . . . cannot afford to have almost one million youths drop out each year only to become unwanted and unemployed" (Schreiber, 1964).

In 1965, Title I of the Elementary and Secondary Education Act was created to distribute funding to schools to help disadvantaged students (Hirschfeld, 2008). Funds were authorized for professional development, instructional materials, resources to support educational programs, and the promotion of parental involvement (Paul, 2017).

Figure 2.1 presents a timeline of other national initiatives in education around this time and since.

In a *USA Today* interview, Michael Casserly, executive director of the Council of the Great City Schools, stated that "the pandemic sparked both an immediate emergency and a slow-motion disaster for disadvantaged students in the United States" (Torres, 2020). In districts that turned to remote instruction, achievement growth was lower for all subgroups, but especially for students attending high-poverty schools (Goldhaber et al., 2022).

Updated data from the KIDS COUNT Data Center show that 14% of U.S. high school students did not graduate on time in 2019–20 (Annie E. Casey Foundation, 2023).

Robert Balfanz, the director of the Everyone Graduates Center at the Johns Hopkins University School of Education, stated, "the graduation flexibility states provided in 2020 'held students harmless' for academic disruptions, but they also may have given educators a false

Figure 2.1

National Education Initiatives

In 1986, the National Dropout Prevention Center was formed. It serves as a clearinghouse on issues related to dropout prevention and offers research-based practices and strategies to increase graduation rates in schools across the United States.
In 1994, the Goals 2000: Educate America Act provided resources to states and communities to develop and implement comprehensive education reforms aimed at helping all students reach challenging academic and occupational skill standards in an attempt to provide both equity and excellence for all students ("What Is Goals 2000," 1994). They stated their goal by the year 2000 would be to have a graduation rate of 90%.
In 2001, the No Child Left Behind Act (NCLB) replaced the Elementary and Secondary Education Act (ESSA). States were required to bring all students at least up to a minimum academic standard on state tests by the 2013–14 school year. By 2015 no states had reached that proficiency level (Klein, 2015).
In 2006, one of the most extensive surveys of American high school dropouts, *The Silent Epidemic: Perspectives of High School Dropouts*, was conducted by Bridgeland, Dilulio, and Morison. Commissioned by the Bill & Melinda Gates Foundation, the primary purpose was to study the dropout problem from a perspective that had not been considered before: by the student dropouts themselves. The results of this survey will be mentioned later in this book.
In 2009, Race to the Top (RTT) funding was introduced by President Obama as a competitive fund to promote school improvement on both a state and local level and turn around struggling schools (Chen, 2022).
In 2015, Congress passed the Every Student Succeeds Act to replace NCLB, allowing states more independence over how they delineate school success and the interventions they use when schools fail to show progress. One of the goals was to reach the highest high school graduation rate on record at 81%, by helping disadvantaged and high-need students (Brown et al., 2016). "It's important to note here that although graduation rates reached a record high of 83% in the 2014–2015 school year, it's difficult to know which states earned this increase in graduation rates through higher standards and which states achieved it through lowered expectations" (Kamenetz & Turner, 2016).
Then in 2019, the COVID-19 pandemic had a negative effect on student learning and the overall dropout rate, especially after schools nationwide shut down (Moscoviz & Evans, 2022).
In 2020–21, two COVID relief packages were distributed to help states cope with the effects of the pandemic. The Governor's Emergency Education Relief Fund was given to states to offer flexibility in directing aid to high-need students (Lieberman, 2022).

sense of security with regard to high school students' progress." State flexibility was intended to be temporary, but students in the subsequent high school classes became more disengaged, not less (Sparks, 2022).

So why hasn't the student dropout rate been significantly reduced in the last six decades? It's reasonable to wonder why, after years of additional federal funding provided to states to address this issue, our nation would not have initiated a more effective solution by now. Unfortunately, so many support personnel in schools continue to be overwhelmed by other demands of their time each day. Many continue to exhaust much of their professional time providing administrative and other non-prevention services in the schools. Too many students in need of more intensive support do not have access to enough individualized encouragement and coping strategies in time to prevent their dropping out of school.

Next, let's take a closer look at the real impact of student dropouts and then examine what can be done to better address this issue.

The Impact of Dropping Out

When students drop out of school, it initiates a gauntlet-like path in life that is enclosed on both sides with hazardous choices and unconsidered outcomes. Their lives usually don't lead even close to a place that they might have envisioned before dropping out. Eventually, a large number of these young people become desperate, needing to rely on public assistance and/or eventually becoming homeless or incarcerated. Consider the following statistics:

- Studies have shown that students who drop out of school are more likely to end up in the criminal justice system (Chilton, 2023; Hale & Canter, 2023). For example, according to the National Center for Education Statistics, about 68% of state prison inmates did not complete high school, and 70% of inmates in federal prisons did not graduate from high school (Truth in American Education, 2023).

- Dropping out of school has dramatic effects on a student's future employment, earnings, health, and overall welfare. According to *Public School Review* (*PSR*), students who drop out of high school are more likely to live a life of cyclic unemployment and have a greater dependence on government assistance than those who graduate from high school or get a GED (Barrington, 2023).

- The American Public Health Association considers school dropouts as "a public health issue because disparities in education predict disparities in health outcomes. Promoting education and its consequent reduction in health disparities could save eight times more lives than medical treatment" (Lansford et al., 2016).

- Dropouts are more likely going to experience a lifetime of increased obstacles and other challenges. In addition to surges of depression and anxiety, there are other negative effects resulting from dropping out of school.

According to Kate Barrington from *PSR* (2023),

- high school dropouts account for 67% of inmates in state prisons and 56% of federal prisons;

- students who drop out of high school earn an average of $670 less per week than students who graduate;

- it's estimated that half of all Americans on public assistance are school dropouts;

- the dropout rate costs our country over $7.3 billion in annual Medicaid spending;

- females 16 to 24 who are high school dropouts are more likely to be, or become, young single mothers; and

- dropouts are more likely to experience a life of sporadic and low-paying employment and higher rate of needing government assistance.

We need to consistently remind students of the many benefits of graduating. Besides providing better job opportunities, there are several other advantages from graduating that students should consider. According to Acceleration Academies (2022), graduating from high school provides the following benefits:

- **Opportunities in school and work**
  More flexibility in the jobs applied for, better chance of going to college, higher chance of being successful, and opens up more possibilities.

- **Connections through school**
  Valuable connections for advice, information, and direction, provides a safe community of professionals and friends.

- **Inspiration to family and friends**
  A sense of accomplishment and opportunity to feel proud,
  encourages more respect from other family members and peers,
  and can provide a role model for them.

- **Increased self-confidence**
  A boost of self-esteem, determination, and perseverance to
  succeed in other areas of life.

My Personal Story

After I left my home in Connecticut, my parents had the police searching
for me for several months. They had no idea that we were living somewhere north of Quebec, Canada, first in our car and then in an abandoned
cabin we found in the middle of a desolate area. I had used my older
sister's birth certificate as my identification to cross the Canadian border.
We sustained ourselves mostly by eating the fish that we caught in a nearby
lake. While there, my boyfriend Kevin became physically abusive, and I was
very afraid. I literally had nowhere to escape to and no one around I could
seek help from. After our money ran out, he decided we would leave
Canada and live somewhere in Vermont.

We arrived in small hippy community on the outskirts of Burlington.
Rather than looking for employment, Kevin pawned personal items to
buy our food. Homeless and starving, we soon found an older guy who
said we could stay at his place for a while. This turned out to be a bad
situation. He was attracted to me, and I was worried for my safety. After
several weeks, a local noticed how young I was and must have realized I
was a runaway and called the police. I was picked up and questioned by
a police officer. Even though I gave him a false name, he said I had to
go to the police station because there was an all-points bulletin (APB)
posted on a runaway that fit my description. We were finally caught! My
parents were contacted and came to "rescue" me. When my boyfriend
found out my parents were on their way to pick me up, he quickly left
the state. I thought maybe I was finally free from him when my parents
arrived. I was actually excited and relieved to see them.

I wish kids could have a glimpse of what life is really like when you drop
out and have no means to support yourself. My decision to drop out
and run away should have taught me a lesson. Instead, I ended up
running away again a few months later.

The Reasons Students Drop Out

3

Many of today's dropouts have been overlooked and have fallen between the cracks. Sometimes school personnel miss the warning signs that could have been recognized and addressed much earlier. School staff often lack the time and/or the necessary supports needed to adequately address enough of the issues that lead to a student dropping out, and there may be insufficient funding available to hire more school support personnel.

Some of the reasons kids drop out are more obvious, while others are obscure and less often addressed by school personnel. The following is a summary of a review of the professional literature on why students drop out, including some of my own personal insights from my experiences. The reasons some students give for wanting to drop out may be surprising, so it's imperative for educators to hear each student's individual story.

Academic Challenges

These difficulties can range from learning disabilities, test anxiety, lack of basic study skills, retention, general anxiety, and feelings of failure. The pandemic has exacerbated these difficulties due to ongoing increased learning loss that is continuing to affect students (Kuhfeld et al., 2022). These perceptions often accumulate and eventually lead to a sense of hopelessness that prevents them from trying to succeed academically in school. Consequently, students shut down their efforts to try, which inevitably leads to even more failure and discouragement. Once a student falls further and further behind academically, it becomes easier to give up than try to catch up.

Disconnection and Disengagement

Disengagement can happen when students do not comprehend what is being taught, do not have others at school with whom they can connect, or have a perception that school personnel do not appreciate or value them. What's the motivation to go to school if students feel disliked or disregarded, or if their school experiences are mostly discouraging? If school personnel cannot motivate these students to graduate, then who will? Sometimes services are available to help them, but many of these students are never connected with these supports (Gewertz, 2022).

Another factor in student disengagement from school comes from the increasingly easy access to the internet. Engaging online is often much easier and more appealing to students than sitting in a classroom listening to a lecture. It's difficult for educators and parents to compete for students' motivation to learn, with the engaging and sometimes addictive nature of online media. We need to work harder and smarter at reengaging our students so they feel invited to drop in instead of drop out. Educators should keep searching for and developing fresh ways to engage students in and outside of the classroom. Figure 3.1 shows a list of resources relating to student engagement.

Chronic Discipline Problems

Students who have a history of acting out in class and/or in other school activities can be labeled by school personnel and others as "troublemakers" or "frequent (discipline) flyers." These students are often unfairly singled-out and blamed for even minor infractions of rules and other expectations and eventually are suspended or expelled for their behavior. Unfortunately, these students may wind up in the criminal justice system instead of receiving the help they truly need. This form of unjust discipline only contributes to the "school-to-prison pipeline" problem that has hurt many of our students (American Civil Liberties Union, 2023).

Lack of School Resources and Supports

All students need help from time to time. If a student does not feel there is anyone at school they can talk with when they need help, they will likely go somewhere else. That help may come from another peer. Whether a student has basic living needs or academic, social, or emotional issues, they could benefit from a connection with at least one caring adult. Students need to feel comfortable going to a support person for help. When this kind of support is not readily available or difficult to find by an individual student, they will be left only to their own resources and experiences. This often does not end well for the student who needs help the most.

Figure 3.1

Student Engagement Resources
• •

Online Resources for StudentEngagement
"How to Increase Student Engagement in the High-School Classroom," by Andrea Banks. *Insights to Behavior* (2023). https://insightstobehavior.com/blog/how-to-increase-student-engagement-in-the-high-school-classroom/
"7 Strategies for Engaging High School Students," by Matthew Whalen. *National Society of High School Scholars* (2023). https://www.nshss.org/resources/blog/blog-posts/how-to-engage-high-school-students-in-active-learning/
"6 Strategies to Engage and Motivate Teenaged Students," by BusyTeacher.org. https://m.busyteacher.org/23290-teen-troubles-engage-motivate-6-strategies.html
"10 Teacher's Tips for Making Teenage Students Excited in the Classroom," by Devon "Fergy" Ferguson. *Teach With Fergy [blog]* (2018). https://teachwithfergy.com/10-teachers-tips-for-making-teenage-students-excited-in-the-classroom/

Books on Student Engagement
Ideas Ideas Ideas: A Collection of Proven Ideas from Education's Front Lines to Improve the Climate and Culture of Your School, by Steven A. Bollar (Josten's Renaissance, 2016).
Motivating Students Who Don't Care: Proven Strategies to Engage All Learners (2nd ed.), by Allen Mendler (Solution Tree Press, 2021).
Reimagining Student Engagement: From Disrupting to Driving, by Amy Elizabeth Berry (Corwin, 2022).
Confronting the Crisis of Engagement: Creating Focus and Resilience for Students, Staff, and Communities, by Douglas B. Reeves, Nancy Frey, & Douglas Fisher (Corwin, 2022).

Technology and Social Media Interference

Today's students are spending increased time entrenched on their digital devices rather than on schoolwork or face-to-face socializing, which can lead to a negative impact on their social and mental well-being. According to a report by the U.S. Surgeon General's Advisory, up to 95% of youth ages 13 to 17 use some form of social media (2023). And it's not just that they are using this technology, it's how they are using it and what they are missing when most of their time is consumed by it.

Technology dependency can inhibit a young person's journey to graduation when it becomes an addiction. With technology there is clearly a "too much." When social media becomes an addiction for some students, it is recommended that they participate in a "digital detox" to reduce the amount of time spent on these digital devices (Hilliard, 2024). Overindulgence in digital devices can distract students from their learning and can misguide them from knowing real facts.

History of Chronic Absenteeism and Truancy

Once students have missed too many days of school and fallen behind academically, they lose sight of any possibility to graduate. Chronic absenteeism can be a more accurate predictor of school failure and dropping out than test scores, especially when the truancy starts as early as sixth grade (Allison & Attisha, 2019). Missing days of academic instruction, the possibility of receiving mental health support, and the loss of connection with friends at school can cause students to increase their thoughts about giving up. Sometimes a student's excuses are authentic, but once it happens repeatedly it becomes a chronic problem that causes them to fall so far behind that they risk being held back. Students who are retained and do not receive individualized help are at a higher risk of dropping out (Giano et al., 2022).

Bullying and School Violence

Children and youth who are vulnerable or ostracized in society tend to be at higher risk for victimization and bullying by their peers, especially if they are one of the few minority students at a mostly white school (Bushnell, 2021). Sadly, bullying is an ongoing issue for many students in today's schools.

It's extremely difficult for a student to focus on their learning when they are being intimidated or threatened by other students at school. If the bullying is not dealt with effectively by school personnel, the students who are victims of bullying might start avoiding coming to school out of fear or anxiety. If nothing happens to stop the bullying, students may feel they need to deal with it themselves. This can lead to violence against others and/or self-harm or suicide. Often, the victims of bullying quietly endure the daily cruelty dealt to them. The impact on them often leads to further discouragement, disengagement, and hopelessness with school. Schools need to be safe and inviting places where our youth feel secure, accepted, encouraged, and helped.

Family Mental and/or Physical Health Issues

Parents play an incredibly important role in their child's life. When a parent or other family member has mental or physical health issues, it affects the entire family. Some everyday stress and anxiety are normal. But raising an adolescent can be an especially challenging task and can sometimes exhaust the coping skills of any parent.

During the pandemic, the challenges of living with teenagers became even more stressful because families were required to stay at home together for long periods of time. The Centers for Disease Control and Prevention (CDC) reported that "adolescents aged 12 to 17 years accounted for the highest proportion of mental health-related emergency room visits in both 2019 and 2020" (Leeb et al., 2020). The disruptions and interruptions of a mental, emotional, or behavioral issue can make it nearly impossible for some students to stay on track academically (McCullough, 2021).

If a child grows up in a dysfunctional family and has experienced several adverse childhood experiences (ACEs), whether emotional or physical, it will increase their risk of developing mental health problems themselves (Gu et al., 2022). Past trauma, feelings of abandonment or hopelessness, and unresolved grief and loss can all contribute to a child's inability to focus on their education. A nurturing home atmosphere provides the foundation for a positive mental well-being (Mphaphuli, 2023; Radevska, 2021).

Young people have a better chance of staying and succeeding in school if they live with families that are functioning in a healthy way. But school personnel have little or no influence over what happens with these students once they are at home. Students who come from dysfunctional homes will need more support from significant others, including caring professionals at school who provide individualized, supportive relationships with these students.

Peer Influence

Peers have a strong influence on middle and high school–aged students. Some students encourage their peers to do well in school and help them work toward graduation. However, there are also peers who can have an adverse influence on students, such as convincing them to cut school, involving them in high-risk behaviors, or encouraging them to drop out. Peers can also develop into boyfriend or girlfriend relationships that become controlling or overbearing.

Some young people understand the issues that influence their peers to drop out. Encouraging these teens to help their peers can be mutually supportive.

Substance Abuse Issues

Developing a sense of belonging is one of our most basic needs and drives. When students feel they don't belong, they can experience enormous stress and/or depression and feelings of hopelessness. Young people are more likely to experience increased social pressure, especially on social media, to act or do things to feel accepted or popular, including using drugs and alcohol (Osbourne, 2023).

Teens who abuse alcohol or drugs tend to have lower grades, increased absences, and are more likely to drop out of school. According to the Drug Enforcement Administration (DEA), high school dropout rates have risen as a result of substance abuse (2023). It's important to determine if substance abuse is a primary cause of a student's chronic absenteeism in order to intervene early and get them the help they need. Substance abuse prevention programs are especially important, and their implementation should start as early as possible.

Language, Racial, and Cultural Disparity

With our increasing population of immigrant students, bilingual education is extremely important if we want to help all students graduate. Schools are sometimes the only place these students can go to seek help, and if there is no program focusing on their unique needs, there is a chance these students will eventually become discouraged and drop out. Racial and cultural disparity continues to exist in public schools. According to the American Psychological Association (APA), "black students continue to receive harsher punishments than white students for the same infractions" (Abrams, 2023). This disparity can impact students' long-term learning and success (Bushnell, 2021). According to the U.S. Department of the Treasury (2023), "the key determinants of many of these disparities are factors outside students' control, including the socioeconomic status of their parents, the schools they attend, the neighborhoods in which they live, discrimination in disciplinary actions, and the race of the teacher to which they are assigned." This has been an ongoing problem that needs to be addressed to ensure that all students, regardless of race or color, receive substantial educational opportunities and possibilities that will increase their success in school.

Extreme Poverty

According to the U.S. Census Bureau, there are 37.9 million people living in poverty in our country (Creamer et al., 2022). Socioeconomic status is a key indicator of a student's risk of dropping out (Barrington, 2023). The Annie E. Casey Foundation reports that nearly 24 million children live in a single-parent home, with most being mother-only households (2022). Single mothers are also more likely to experience poverty. The stress related to poverty is overwhelming and at times seems impossible to overcome.

Students who are raised in poverty face challenges beyond a lack of resources. According to the American Psychological Association (APA), students living in poverty experience mental and physical issues at a much higher rate than those living above the poverty line (APA, 2022). Growing up in poverty gives students a huge disadvantage since many live in low socioeconomic neighborhoods and deal with the day-to-day struggles to just survive, like inadequate housing, lack of nutrition, increased threat of violence, lack of resources, and more.

If poverty is a main contributing factor to students dropping out, school districts need to ensure adequate supports are in place to help these students and their families. I myself experienced what it was like to raise children while living in poverty. The constant emotional and mental strain is sometimes unbearable. Schools can provide parents with a list of community resources on their school's website and in the counseling office. Poverty is a vicious cycle, and the only way to break the cycle is through education and intervention. Our states need to do more to help those living in poverty find a way out.

Pregnancy

Teen pregnancy and teen parenting contribute greatly to high school dropout rates among girls.

According to the National Conference of State Legislatures (NCSL; 2018), 30% of teenage girls who drop out of high school cite pregnancy or parenthood as a primary reason. Among those who have a baby before age 18, about 40% finish high school. Unfortunately, the children of teen parents are at a higher risk of becoming teen parents themselves (Hendrick & Maslowsky, 2019).

Although there are not as many pregnant teens at school as there were a decade ago (Wildsmith et al., 2022), we still need to address this issue, since many of these girls are in need of additional help in parenting skills, their own mental well-being, and furthering their education/career skills. Otherwise, they will continue to be dependent on government assistance and may never discover a way to break the cycle of poverty. I remember struggling with my own issues as a teen mom. It was difficult trying to live an adult life with family responsibilities while being a teenager and living on my own. Having access to a mentor, parenting classes, continued education, counseling, assistance from agencies that can help with housing—all these resources can help a young teen parent. There is a plethora of organizations today that can assist teen parents, and with the use of the internet, they are easier to access. Schools need to have this information readily available to teens who are either pregnant or who are already raising a child.

Lack of Grit and Fostering Resiliency and a Self-Encouraging Mindset

We have lost something valuable over the years that our children desperately need today. Our earlier generations taught their children, often through role modeling, the critical importance of grit and perseverance. When invited, today's elders enjoy sharing stories of how difficult it was "back then" and how families struggled to make ends meet during very difficult circumstances. Their resiliency enabled them and their families to survive and thrive through difficulties in their lives. Many of our children today have not been instilled with enough of this drive. They give up far too quickly when circumstances become frustrating, challenging, or boring.

In this fast-paced generation that we live in, many of our young people want instant results and do not see the value in working at long-term goals. Instant gratification rules their motivation. In her book *Grit*, Angela Duckworth researched passion and perseverance and suggested that the personal strength of grit, which she defines as perseverance and passion, might be the best predictor of academic success and a healthier emotional life (2016). She found many cases where people who had more of this characteristic achieved significantly greater personal successes in their lives. She includes a 12-item Grit Scale that students can take to measure their level of grit. Students learn grit and perseverance when they face difficulties or challenges and adults need to resist the urge to instantly intervene. If young people are always rescued from challenges, they will miss an opportunity to learn how to be resilient or the importance of perseverance. This can create a dependance on looking to others to be rescued every time there is an obstacle in their way.

Having an encouraging mindset can be a problem for those students who easily give up on school and themselves. Instilling an encouraging mindset starts early in childhood and needs to be refreshed throughout a person's life span. When children constantly see themselves as failures or disappointments, they set themselves up for failure and are prone to not see a way forward when facing difficulties. Students can learn how to reframe their self-doubt and negative thinking into more positive growth mindset statements. They can focus on "I can" statements rather than "I can't" and learn how to be mindful of their emotions and thoughts. This mindset shift can turn around a student who has only experienced failure in their life.

Desire for More Personal Freedom

A desire for freedom is not mentioned in any of my research I found on why students drop out. Nevertheless, it seems to be an important reason to consider here. Part of normal development of teenagers is to strive for greater independence. "I just want to be free!" is a reason some students give for dropping out of school. If it wasn't present, some teens would want to live at home with their parents indefinitely. This need for freedom may be driven by a teen's personal life and what they are currently dealing with at home that makes attending school difficult for them. For me, I left home because of the strain of living with a parent who suffered from mental illness and having a difficult time getting along with my mother. Some teens have to endure physical or emotional abuse while trying to attend school. Maybe there is such a financial strain on the family that the teen needs to work a job to help pay the bills while going to school. These reasons are not in the student's control. They drop out to be free from the stress and fear of living at home or the burden of having to care for family members. Some will end up joining gangs to find a sense of belonging for what they believe is love and acceptance. Although they can't see a way out, there are other options for them—with the right kind of help.

There are youngsters, however, who just want to be free from the rules and authority of home and school. Some teens are able to resist this drive or at least hang in there until they graduate. Other students, in particular those with issues that discourage them from staying in school and entice them to leave school, eventually become driven with an overwhelming motivation to "just get out of this place" (school). Without carefully considering the likely long-term consequences, they impulsively drop out. Unfortunately, once they drop out of school, the personal freedom they are seeking is often short-lived. They eventually discover that the freedom they were seeking becomes difficult to maintain. Life eventually brings new responsibilities and stresses. Without at least a high school diploma, they will likely discover that coping and dealing with personal life challenges will be even more difficult.

My Personal Story

My reasons for dropping out of school had to do with so many risk factors. First, I had a learning disability since elementary school that caused me to struggle academically. I was also dealing with many mental health issues at home. My dad was in and out of mental institutions and my sister, just a few years older than me, almost died from a self-inflicted gunshot wound. I took my stress and insecurities out on my mother and became very defiant. I started sneaking out of my home at night and became incorrigible.

I did not feel connected to anything or anyone and started skipping school in fourth grade. I was never asked by anyone at school why I left home in the first place, whether I missed going to school, or why I stopped seeing my friends. I was experiencing very low self-worth and self-confidence. At times, I wanted to be free from the stress of my home life. I lacked the grit to be assertive in my relationship with my boyfriend, but at the same time I didn't know how to express my feelings of sadness and confusion. This caused me to place all my trust in a mentally unstable boyfriend, which led to a lifelong decision—dropping out—for which I was not prepared.

Remember, these are just some of the reasons students have for dropping out of school. There are many more underlying factors to consider than just focusing on one or two reasons. This means schools need to have a comprehensive approach to dropout prevention that takes into account each individual student and that particular student's needs. This list of common reasons can be used to gain support from stakeholders in your community. There is also much we can learn from the students themselves, especially those who have dropped out. Their stories need to be heard and considered when confronting the dropout crisis.

What We Can Learn From Students

4

This chapter will provide recommendations for how schools can improve their effectiveness in preventing students from dropping out based on what these students tell us. Some of these ideas might seem obvious. However, it can be helpful to take a fresh look at what is being done, what could be done better, and what unique insights and/ or interventions could be especially helpful to the students in your school. Since there are multiple risk factors involved with students who drop out, schools need a multilayered, comprehensive approach to reaching these students and it needs to start early to really make a difference (Lee-St. John et al., 2018).

First, this chapter will provide insights from students who were on the verge of dropping out but didn't and also from students who eventually did drop out. This can help us to gain some perspective on what caused these students to make this life-altering decision. Second, I explore some additional critical insights and potential strategies that school personnel could consider. Included in this chapter is a screening tool to help identify students who are at a higher risk for dropping out. This survey-type tool can help provide necessary information about areas where these students may need additional support. Included is a list of possible interventions to consider in our efforts to keep these students in school.

What We Can Learn From Students Who Almost Dropped Out

The following four stories are about students who, after making the decision to drop out, attended a dropout recovery program. I chose these examples so you can consider what it was that changed their mind. It's important to think about whether their change in mindset was due to initiatives or efforts that could be helpful for you to consider when encouraging students who dropped out to continue their education and graduate.

Alyssa had always been a gifted student, earning good grades in advanced courses and delighting in discussing the fine points of history and other subjects with teachers and classmates alike. Then, in the final semester of her senior year in 2020, the COVID-19 pandemic changed everything. She recalls, "We went out on spring break and never came back."

At first, she dutifully logged on every day to participate in online courses. But she missed walking into school each day and calling out "good morning" to friends and educators, missed the stimulating conversations in class, and missed the opportunity to seek out a teacher for one-on-one guidance when needed. Although just months away from graduating with her class, Alyssa dropped out. She had a good job as a line cook, bought herself a car, and felt she had found her career path as a chef. But still, one thing nagged at her: what about that diploma?

Then, one day, she received a phone call from a representative of Acceleration Academies. This person offered her a flexible, personalized alternative path to graduation. "Two years go by and then I get a phone call," recalls Alyssa. "I was really excited by that phone call. I didn't just want to settle for a GED. I wanted to get my diploma." That excitement only grew when she enrolled as one of the academy's first graduation candidates at this location. The academy welcomed her with warm smiles and steady encouragement. "They were so nice, so open, so welcoming," Alyssa says. "I just had to give it a shot."

Barely two months into her studies, Alyssa suffered another setback—a serious car accident that required her to go to the doctor several times a week and made it hard for her to make it to campus every day. But just as her momentum began to sag, the academy team stepped up. They told her she could work online when she couldn't make it onsite, and they urged her to reach for her dreams. "They believed in me. They said, 'you can do this,'" she says. "I needed support, and they really gave me the support."

Alyssa works full-time in the evenings, and she said this school's scheduling flexibility meant she could work with educators before her shift and then log on to do more coursework afterwards. "That's what made it hard for me to go back to traditional school," she says. "I had already started my career choice, started making money, started my life."

She has plans to go to culinary school, to be head chef in a restaurant, and someday to own her own place. But first, she has the chance to savor her walk across the stage to collect her diploma wearing a bow tie she and her brother—who also graduated this year, from another school—shared. "It felt magical," she says. "My grandmother said, 'You had the biggest smile in the world. Don't trade it for anything else,'" she recalls. "And to think, it might not have happened."

"If it weren't for that phone call, I would still be wondering how I could get my diploma," marvels Alyssa. "I find it unbelievable still that Acceleration Academies contacted me. It was like fate."

Insights

It can make a difference to just reach out personally with care, encouragement, and interest to a student who is on the edge of dropping out. If someone from Acceleration Academies had not contacted and encouraged Alyssa, she might not have believed that receiving a diploma was even possible for her. Many students just need someone to personally reach out to them and connect on a personal level. Alyssa's mentor helped encourage her and kept her accountable.

(Used with permission from Acceleration Academies)

Raynard moved around to different neighborhoods about once a year.

I would find friends and then quickly lose them when we moved again. Looking back, I always found myself around bad stuff, including gang violence. The low point was getting shot four times when I was 16. I couldn't attend school while recovering, and by the end of the year, it hit me that I would fail ninth grade. That life-changing incident spurred me to drop out. I came from a good family, but dropping out was a common occurrence among those around me, so it didn't seem like a big deal at the time.

After spending nearly four years not doing much with my life, I was tired of doing the wrong things and I wanted something better for my life. So, I drew on my courage and went back to school. I still remember the fear I felt before my first day at Excel. Voices around me and in my own head told me I was too old to

(Continued)

(Continued)

be in high school. I had to put that aside. I couldn't let how others felt about me or my past decisions determine my future.

At this new school, the teachers and staff didn't give up on me and always pushed me to improve. If my classmates or I got a C, they helped us work toward a B, and then toward an A. Having someone in my corner felt good. I had been holding myself back without realizing it.

The experience changed everything for me. Today, I work with Excel students who have been placed in out-of-home care. If we want to reach the individuals who need us most, it's critical we share our stories. Telling students about my rocky path to a high school diploma, for example, helps them relate and open up to me.

To be able to say "I can help you" is the reason I get up every day and come to work. The most rewarding thing is to see the students I've mentored graduate from high school. I understand the difficult and often traumatic experiences they overcame to get that diploma and reach for a better life. Together we work on developing coping and problem-solving skills. And a big part of my role is listening and making sure the students feel heard.

(Used with permission from Excel High School)

Insights

It can be very difficult for young people who have experienced traumatic setbacks to return to school and graduate. When Raynard decided to not let his past decisions affect his future, he was able to move forward. This mind shift happened when he realized he was stuck and not moving ahead in his life. This perception is fundamental for helping a student to become motivated to make life changes and move forward with new goals and initiatives. Ideally, it would have been better if he was reached out to prior to leaving school in the first place. Excel not only invited him to come back to school, but they also provided the acceptance and support he needed to move forward. Providing one-to-one academic help was crucial for Raynard, who had missed months of school. He felt encouraged by his teachers and it gave him a new sense of purpose and drive. I wish more stories ended like his, becoming a mentor to help encourage and work with other students who need help.

Janice liked school until she reached high school. There was no specific trigger that led her to quit school. She simply felt it was less and less important in her life. Being "good" in school was not the problem. She had good grades, friends, even tried a few extracurricular activities. While attending school, she was able to work a job and live independently. Some may think that working, paying the bills, and living independently could overwhelm a student. Not Janice. Being overwhelmed was not her problem. She simply never felt part of the school culture. She always thought there had to be more to this. But what was it? She could not put her finger on it. She just believed school did not really matter in her life. Like many students who lose interest in school, there was no safety net, nobody to even notice she was struggling. No one noticed any signs—until she finally dropped out.

However, despite what she had thought, someone had noticed her. That someone was a teacher who was surprised that this capable young woman was no longer in school. She reached out to Janice and asked her if she would be interested in attending The Synergy School. This school was described as having a caring and friendly environment where everyone helped students be their best. At first, Janice was skeptical. Based on her experience with school, she found it difficult to believe that anybody, especially people in school, would care if she attended or not. Regardless, the teacher convinced Janice to consider it and Janice enrolled.

From the start, Janice was surprised at the interest shown in her by the staff. It was not just the teachers, it was everyone. Paraprofessionals, administrators, and security personnel all acknowledged her. Her biggest surprise was the acceptance. Instructionally, the lessons were laid out, and she was always expected to do her work. That was just like in her old high school. What made this experience different was the honest, authentic interaction. She said, "People really cared about you. They really wanted you to come to school. They really wanted you to be successful. They really cared if you did the work."

She soon realized that this place was different from any school she had gone to in the past. There was more interaction with the staff. She found herself immersed in support, affirmation, and encouragement. When she struggled, there was always someone to guide her and offer support. She always knew that ultimately she was responsible for her success or failure. Everyone she worked with reinforced this in her and in all the other students. Responsibility was a universal expectation for everyone. She described it as

(Continued)

(Continued)

"every kid was at the center of their work," "every student felt like they were important," and "all the students felt like they belonged."

With a sharp focus on her future, Janice graduated and continued working and living in the community. Today, she continues to be successfully employed and lives independently in her own house. She purchased her own home and pays a mortgage. Clearly, the grit, determination, and sense of purpose instilled by these powerful educators has made an important difference in Janice's life.

(Used with permission from Synergy Public School)

Insights

Here is a case where a student was doing well in school, was responsible, had friends, and seemed to be on track to graduate. Sometimes it is difficult to notice these students because school personnel tend to focus more on those who are either excelling or struggling. Since Janice did not fit the usual signs of a potential dropout, her lack of interest in school went unnoticed. One teacher noticed that Janice had left school and reached out to her and encouraged her to try an alternative program; Janice was at first skeptical. However, with caring determination, this teacher finally convinced Janice to give it a try. She immediately discovered this school to be different from any school she ever attended. The people were caring and made her feel important. This school helped her feel a sense that she belonged there. Janice credited her success in school and life to the grit, determination, and sense of purpose that was instilled in her by these powerful educators.

 Doug had always felt he had the strengths to make it in school, but he did not connect within the large, comprehensive high school setting. Learning was too impersonal, instructional relationships lacked personality, and purpose and meaning in his studies eventually evaporated. He did not feel that school had any point. He became lost, frustrated, and discouraged. This highly intelligent student eventually became a statistic—a dropout.

As a last-ditch effort, his school counselor reached out to Doug and told him about the Synergy School, an in-district alternative school for struggling students. He figured, "Why not—what do I have to lose?"

He made the decision to enroll and quickly became immersed in the caring, compassionate learning environment he describes as "familial." Doug appreciates the genuine teaching style of the staff, who stressed that learning was not solely academic. Here, teachers and administrators focused on academics and stressed life lessons of responsibility, accountability, and perseverance. They emphasized that this was a place in which Doug had a chance to start over. Expectations were not based on a student's prior history but on the future possibilities inside each of them. Doug found himself surrounded by students who struggled just like him, and caring staff who made him feel like he belonged. He felt respected and appreciated and soon committed to the work ahead.

There was no negative judgment, just positive affirmation that ignited a belief in himself to rise above previous setbacks. He mentions a particular principal who once posed the question: "I know who they say you are, but who do you say you are?" That question stayed with him as he attempted to take control of his future and carve out his own identity. This young man who had dropped out of school eventually graduated and enlisted in the Marine Corps. He served as a platoon sergeant for six years. He then went on to join the Connecticut National Guard where he completed his work in flight school, graduating as a UH-Blackhawk pilot. His success there culminated in his promotion to pilot and flight instructor for 16 years. Following the end of his 22-year career from the Armed Services, United Airlines employed him, where he currently works flying 737s around the globe.

On occasion, Doug returns to the Synergy School to share his success with students who are experiencing their own challenges with school and life. He has also spoken in public forums like the Town Council and the Board of Education to extol the positive educational influence and impact that caring, passionate, and dedicated educators can have on students who have lost their way in school.

(Used with permission from Synergy Public School)

Insights

Doug was a very capable student. Unfortunately, he became lost, frustrated, and discouraged. He gave several reasons for losing interest in school. For him, the school staff were too impersonal and he lost the sense of purpose and meaning in his studies. When he became so discouraged that he did not see the point in finishing school, Doug's school counselor reached out to him and invited him to learn about an alternative program and give it a try. Having someone at his school care enough to reach out to him must have sent the message that he mattered. Doug finally found a program that fit his needs and a place where he felt respected and appreciated. When an administrator asked him the question, "who do you say you are?" it had a lasting impact on him. It challenged him to take control of his future and carve out his own identity.

Insights From Students After They Dropped Out

We can learn much from students after they drop out of school. Their personal experiences can provide insights that can be valuable to professionals who work with at risk young people.

A Landmark Study

In my review of the professional literature, the most recent study conducted with student dropouts that I could find was from 2006. This groundbreaking study in the United States included high school students who had dropped out of school. Titled *The Silent Epidemic: Perspectives of High School Dropouts*, this study was conducted by Bridgeland, Dilulio, Burke, and Morison, with the support of the Bill & Melinda Gates Foundation. The researchers surveyed nearly 470 dropouts, aged 16 to 25, who left high school before earning their diplomas.

The study consisted of a survey designed to obtain a more in-depth look at who these young people were, why they dropped out of high school, and what they believe might have helped them complete their high school education. The following are some of their most relevant recommendations to schools:

- Make school more relevant and engaging to students' interests and lives.

- Provide more opportunities for real-world learning (internships, service-learning projects, and other opportunities).

- Improve access to supports outside of classes.

- Ensure that students have a strong relationship with at least one adult in the school.

- Improve the communication between parents and schools.

- Have teachers notice and acknowledge students more.

- Provide more after-school tutoring.

Insights

Though some or all these recommendations might seem obvious to today's educators, many school personnel have felt overtasked by the stresses of their day-to-day challenges that it is easy to overlook some or many of them. It is important for educators to self-assess how their school is dealing with each of these areas listed according to the population of students being served. Student dropouts themselves sometimes have unique and insightful ideas to help schools improve their effectiveness in reducing or eliminating student dropouts.

Recommended Strategies

Although the strategies recommended in this study were from more than a decade ago, they continue to be relevant today. We must also account for the massive changes young people face with the increased influence of digital social media. Additional recommendations I suggest for today's schools would include

- teaching SEL in all classrooms,

- individual and small group support,

- awareness of and interventions for bullying and other forms of harassment,

- increased school-wide mental health awareness,

- implementing mentoring and peer helping programs, and

- increased supportive interactions in the classroom.

Personal Stories From School Dropouts

Everyone has a life story that is unique depending on their experiences and interactions with others. When a student drops out of school there are usually a combination of factors associated with their decision, but many of their stories go unheard and unnoticed.

My Personal Story

After returning home from running away, I was enrolled in high school even though I never completed the eighth grade. Unfortunately, no one at the school met with me prior to starting. I was expected to just "fit in" with the rest of the students who passed the eighth grade. None of my teachers or other staff there ever met with me to check if I needed any help. Kevin, my boyfriend, also returned home. I was afraid to talk to anyone about my feelings toward Kevin because he would become very angry and unpredictable if he knew I had talked to anyone about him. His controlling and emotionally abusive behavior meant there would be repercussions. So right away I started to disengage with school and did not talk to anyone while there.

Without anyone encouraging me to stay there, I lasted about a week in high school before I started skipping school again. Cutting school was the only thing I knew how to do well. After arriving at school, I would walk off campus and meet up with Kevin. We would either go to his house since his dad was usually not there or hang out where we couldn't be seen by anyone. It wasn't that I didn't like being at school; I was afraid of making friends there. Kevin was afraid of me talking to someone about him. When I was absent from school, someone from school would call my mother. When she confronted me about this, I would just lie. She tried grounding me to the home, but I would just sneak out of the house. Eventually she didn't feel she had much control over me, and we stopped communicating.

One day Kevin showed up at my house with a car. I was shocked that he would come to my home unannounced, and I was surprised to see he had a car. Up to now he had been living homeless in a tobacco barn. I walked outside to see why he was there. He told me, "We are leaving today to live in another state where no one will find us." I was caught off guard and didn't know what to say. I didn't even have time to run back into the house and grab any of my things or say goodbye to my sister, who I was just talking to inside the kitchen. I just left with the clothes on my back. I really wished someone could have stopped me or offered me another alternative, but that never happened and I felt it was too late. I felt like I was stuck in a mentally unstable relationship and had no idea where we were going or if and when I would see my family again. This decision would impact the rest of my life. But the rest of my story will come later in this book.

Insights

Too many young people like me fall through the cracks at school and end up leaving because they feel stuck in a miserable situation and don't know what else they could do. Unchecked anxiety, depression, and/or discouragement can eventually lead to a sense of desperation. This, in turn, can result in personal vulnerability, poor judgment, and sometimes devastating decisions.

Recommended Strategies

No child should go unnoticed in school. Every student should know at least one adult who supports them and with whom they can comfortably talk with. If I had one caring adult who showed an interest in my life, I might have chosen another path than the one I followed. This supportive person could have helped me gain the sense of self-confidence, esteem and resiliency I desperately needed.

I often wonder what might have happened if someone had encouraged me earlier when I started experiencing trouble. If I had someone like a peer helper or mentor to connect with me before I became very discouraged, it may have changed any thoughts I had about giving up on school. Perhaps this person could have helped me understand and tap my strengths to find new ways to cope with issues at home and feel more connected in school. It might have helped if the school encouraged me to be involved in a group or initiative at the school. More important, this person might have been able to encourage me to believe that I had potential and could find ways to feel successful in school.

Since middle school was an intensely transitional time for me, including the issues going on at home, I needed more emotional support from someone in the school, like a counselor or social worker. It would have helped if I also had individualized academic help that could have prevented me from repeating the fourth grade. I believe that interventions are more effective when they are started with students at a younger age. Many dropout predictors are observable and should be addressed at an early age. For example, as a child I started showing signs of chronic absenteeism, low grades, family mental health issues, and withdrawal from school. These risk factors could have been addressed while I was still in elementary school.

Story #1: Disconnected Josh

 Growing up, Josh was a quiet child and had difficulty making friends. Once he started playing video games, he preferred to stay at home where he could play his games with others he met online. That is where he felt accepted and able to connect with others. Once he entered his sophomore year in high school, Josh kept to himself and did not hang out with other students. He did not find sports or any other clubs or activities interesting. He only looked forward to connecting with his virtual friends online.

One day he was approached by several students who started saying mean things about his clothes. He ignored them the best he could, but it kept getting worse until they started saying cruel things about him personally. When he tried talking to one of his teachers about it, he was advised to not let it bother him since these students were just looking for attention and trying to persuade him to react. Josh did not feel understood and did not know who else to talk to about his feelings. His parents expected him to do well in school, and he didn't want to bother them with this issue because he was afraid they would overreact and go to the school principal and make matters worse. So, he talked to his only friends he knew, his online friends.

The advice he received from them was to get back at his bullies. He didn't want to follow their advice and became even more confused about what to do. He just wanted this harassment to stop. His anxiety grew throughout the year, and he eventually started to leave school some days to go back home to play his games. This was easy to do because both of his parents had jobs and weren't around to find out. His grades started dropping as well. His skipping school became a chronic problem, and a school administrator contacted his parents about it. His parents were furious and became verbally harsh toward him. They didn't explore the reasons behind his school avoidance. They just took away his video games for two weeks. Because he was so far behind in his classes, he didn't pass the ninth grade. This resulted in him becoming more discouraged and eventually dropping out of school.

Insights

Josh desperately needed connection with at least one adult at school. He also needed help finding new friends. He missed out on being connected early on with other students through activities, clubs, or other extracurricular offerings. He unfortunately lacked social skills needed for developing friendships. He also lacked self-regulation skills, which could have helped him better regulate his time gaming. It's unfortunate that he did not feel enough of a connection at school and received more support at home while playing his games. The bullying pushed him even further into wanting to leave school and eventually drop out.

Recommended Strategies

- Involve Josh in some activities to get to know other students better (for example, a small group that teaches social and emotional learning [SEL] skills, provide a list of clubs that might hold his interest and help him take a first step in trying one out).

- Provide Josh with a mentor or peer helper or, better yet, give him the opportunity to become a helper himself.

- Make him a member of a small group of students that focuses on improving self-regulation insights and skills.

- Keep adding to your library of self-regulation resources that can be shared with Josh and with his parents or guardians.

- Include activities that help the student improve physical, social, and emotional self-regulation (for example, ask questions like "what would you do if_____?" and practice discussing good and bad choices and big deals versus little deals).

- Explore anger buttons and temper control.

- Practice mindfulness and other calming techniques.

- Brainstorm other options for when all else fails with self-regulation.

- Have a clear understanding of actionable steps that can be taken when being bullied in different situations.

Story #2: Disinterested Shyanne

 Shyanne grew up in a single-family home raised by her mother. She was diagnosed with ADHD early in life. She had abundant energy and a need to be constantly physically active. Her biological father was intermittently involved in her life until she was about eight years old. He never visited her again after that. She experienced behavior problems that started in preschool, which led to difficulty getting along with other children. This continued through elementary school and kept her from focusing on her schoolwork. She was frequently referred for discipline problems. Her mom took her to a doctor who tried different medications to help with her impulsivity, but none of these seemed to help and just caused her to become more agitated. She gravitated toward other students who also experienced trouble in school.

Shyanne's impulsive behavior continued into middle school and progressed into verbal and physical altercations with other students and teachers. Within a few months after beginning high school, she was expelled and placed in an alternative school. She continued to have difficulty paying attention in class and getting along with other students. By now she started smoking pot and hanging out with teens who had been involved in the juvenile court system. Her mom didn't know what else she could do to help her. Eventually, Shyanne was expelled from alternative school and then later expelled from adult education. She finally officially dropped out of school at age 16 and was arrested for evading the police and weapon possession. Shyanne was under house arrest but did not see her probation officer on a regular basis. Besides a few counseling sessions, there were no other interventions or supports offered to her or her mom. Then, in her late teens, she was not able to keep a job for more than a few weeks at a time. Shyanne constantly struggled to survive on her own and had no interest in continuing her education or receiving a GED. She continually searched for others to depend upon for financial support.

Insights

From the very start of her problems in preschool, Shyanne needed help with social and emotional skills. Growing up in a single-parent home added to the risk factors. She would have benefited from one-on-one instruction and being assigned a counselor or social worker to build a supportive relationship with her. She needed a positive peer experience at a young age but lacked appropriate social skills. With all her physical energy it might have helped her to be involved in organized sports. Instead of being suspended from school, she may have benefited from a restorative approach to her discipline problems.

Recommended Strategies

- Provide one-to-one academic help along with strategies for helping her with focusing skills.

- Involve Shyanne in a small support group in elementary school as well as middle school where she can learn SEL skills and role-play these skills in a small group setting.

- Provide a mentor or peer helper to work with her on her impulsive behavior and academic struggles.

- Encourage her to become involved in interests that fit her personal strengths. A mentor or peer can have a positive influence on her applying her personal strengths to different opportunities offered at school.

- Connect her to one caring adult at the school who can be available when she is experiencing problems to prevent her from future suspensions.

- Involve her in a restorative circle where she has an opportunity to find support from others and talk about the causes of her behavior and what she could do differently.

- A school counselor or social worker can reach out to her mom to discover what additional help she needs, including referring her to support services for her and her daughter.

Story #3: Overwhelmed Jose

 Jose was a high achiever and always received As and Bs in all his school subjects. He was enrolled in advanced classes since elementary school and was a well-behaved, respectful student who was liked by his teachers. However, while in 10th grade Jose found out his parents were thinking of separating. He was distressed but tried to not show his feelings while at school. No one in his

(Continued)

(Continued)

school was aware of the constant distress and domestic violence between his parents that Jose often witnessed. He became distracted at school and not as engaged in his classes that he previously once enjoyed. One of his teachers noticed this change in his behavior and asked him if everything was okay, but he responded that he was just tired. Unfortunately, his grades started to drop because he stopped turning in his homework on time.

Jose's dad moved to another state. Jose was devastated and unsure of what this meant for his future. His mom was also struggling emotionally and financially. He felt he needed to now become the man of the house and take care of her, so he started a job after school. This made it even more difficult for Jose to keep up with his schoolwork. He became so far behind in his classes that he decided to drop out as soon as he was old enough and work full time. Jose had hopes of going to college one day but felt this was not a possibility now.

Insights

As soon as Jose's routine behavior started to change, he needed to connect with a school counselor. It is easy to assume that if a student is academically gifted and well-behaved, everything must be fine with them. A caring adult in school might have had a chance to provide the encouraging connection that he needed. Jose did not reach out to even his peers about what he was going through. Sometimes students who appear quiet can be experiencing more stress than students who act out all the time. It's important to notice these changes in a student's behavior; if they do not want to talk about it, refer this student to a caring support person at the school.

Recommended Strategies

- After noticing a change in Jose's behavior, match him with a mentor or student peer helper. A trusting relationship with a mentor or peer could increase the chances of him opening up about his personal struggles.

- Allow time either before class or during exploratory to have students talk about issues or other concerns. This can provide opportunities for students like Jose to open up.

- Refer him to a school counselor or social worker who can meet with his mother and recommend outside help, such as counseling.

- Provide one-to-one academic help with Jose so he can keep up with his schoolwork.

- If needed, explore alternative options for him to keep up with his studies, such as online school.

- Involve Jose in a divorce group, where he can experience support from others going through similar situations.

Story #4: "Hopeless" Jaylyn

 Jaylyn was a senior at her high school and seen by other students as physically attractive and popular. Some girls envied her for that. She had a few close friends and always seemed happy around them. She did well academically and athletically, so she joined the girls' lacrosse team. Although she would never invite anyone to her home, she loved spending time at other friends' homes. She was a very private person when it came to talking about her family, so she avoided conversations that were too personal. She unfortunately heard that a rumor was going around that she was sexually active with several guys even though it was untrue. She didn't know how else to deal with this other than trying to ignore it. She became very depressed and felt alone.

When there was an open house or teacher conference night, Jaylyn never had anyone come to the school. When her teachers asked how they could meet with her parents, she would give excuses for why they couldn't come. She was good at keeping her home life secret until one day when she did not come to school and her friends wondered why she was not there. Jaylyn wasn't responding to any of their text messages. The last message they saw from her on social media was a very alarming message about how she just wanted to end the pain. A couple of girls tried to contact her, but she didn't answer her phone. The next day students were all called into the auditorium for a morning announcement. One of the school counselors announced how sad they were to learn that Jaylyn had an "accident" and unfortunately did not survive. They said they and others would be available for anyone who needed to talk. Students later discovered that Jaylyn was found hanging in her closet by her grandmother, the person who had been raising her. By the time she found her, it was too late. Tragically, she not only dropped out of school but also from life.

Insights

To others it appeared that Jaylyn had a wonderful life. However, she was actually secretly suffering emotionally from the loss of her mother, who had died suddenly earlier that year. She was still grieving while trying to live a different life around her friends to distract her from the reality of what she was actually dealing with internally. Jaylyn was trying to cope with her unresolved grief and loss by pretending to be very happy around her friends and through seeking out attention from boys. The fact that she rarely wanted friends to go to her home and that she never had parents come to school events were indicators that there was likely more to her story. The most alarming sign that something was desperately wrong was when she posted the message about wanting to end the pain. Unfortunately, her kind of tragedy has increasingly become more common in schools, with young people's growing mental health issues. It's easy to miss the warning signs of someone who is deeply depressed. Jaylyn dropped out permanently—from her school and from the rest of her life because she thought her situation was hopeless. This could have been prevented if there had been someone who had noticed, taken the time to listen, discovered what was going on in her life, and then provided or arranged for an ongoing intervention.

Recommended Strategies

- Provide training with students and school staff in "red flags" that indicate that a student could be depressed or at risk of hurting themselves. The night before she was found by her grandmother, Jaylyn posted online how she wanted the pain to stop. This was unusual for her. Unfortunately, her friends didn't recognize just how deeply depressed she was. Students also need to be trained in what to look for online that could be a cry for help and what to do if they see a disturbing message from a peer and are not able to contact them.

- Offer opportunities before class where students have an opportunity to share the struggles and situations that cause them to be anxious or discouraged. Students need to be able to share their concerns and realize that their temporary pain is not a hopeless situation.

- When a student does not have a parent or guardian to attend teacher-parent conferences or other events, check in with that student individually or ask a counselor or social worker to do so.

Sometimes just asking a student directly if everything is okay can provide helpful information, if the student is willing to share.

- Have the appropriate school personnel make a home visit after not receiving any response from home. Conducting home visits can provide the needed information for how to help that parent and student.

- Provide training to students about the effects of bullying on others and what to do if they ever hear of a student being bullied.

- Start a mental health awareness group or club at your school. Address other mental health issues including suicide prevention either in grade-level assemblies or in individual classes. It is important to not only provide information but to allow students to share if they or someone they know is dealing with stressful situations, loss, or any other distress. When addressing the school in an assembly setting, it is important to make sure there are counselors available for students to talk to and be sure to have a follow-up back in the classrooms as an attempt to reach all students. There are many online resources to address suicide prevention in your school. Have this information easily available to students.

Suicide Prevention Resource Center: www.sprc.org
email: info@sprc.org
Phone: 877-GET-SPRC (438-7772)
Text: 988

Society for the Prevention of Teen Suicide: www.sptsusa.org/teens

Trevor Project: www.thetrevorproject.org

Bullycide: https://www.overcomebullying.org/bullycide.html

Your Life Your Voice from Boys Town Hotline: www.yourlifeyourvoice.org

Connect With a Suicide & Crisis Counselor
Text HOME to 741741
www.crisistextline.org/

Strategies to Reach Students at Risk of Dropping Out

5

The following considerations are based on the barriers that can eventually lead to students dropping out. These challenges need to be addressed if our goal is to eliminate as many of these barriers as possible to help keep students on the path to graduation. My hope is that you can gain some new insights and ideas for addressing dropout prevention in your school.

Addressing Students' Mental Health Needs

Our country is experiencing a serious mental health crisis. State legislatures and school districts are responding to a major surge of mental health issues in our young people. Schools throughout the country are overcome with students struggling with mental health issues (Chatterjee, 2022). Sadly, suicide has become the second-leading cause of death for people ages 10 to 34 and accounts for about one death every 11 minutes (Centers for Disease Control and Prevention [CDC], 2021).

According to the National Center for Education Statistics (NCES; 2022), data have shown that since the COVID-19 pandemic, 76% of schools have reported an increase in staff expressing concerns about their students exhibiting depression, anxiety, and trauma.

Many young people feel hopeless and empty and don't know where to turn. The CDC's Youth Risk Behavior Surveillance System (YRBSS) survey provided the following insights (2023a):

- Forty-two percent of high school students felt persistently sad or hopeless almost every day for at least two weeks, with female students (nearly 60%) and LGBQ+ students (nearly 70%) reporting the highest percentages.

* Twenty-nine percent of high school students experienced poor mental health during the past 30 days.

* More than 1 in 5 (22%) students seriously considered attempting suicide and 1 in 10 (10%) attempted suicide one or more times during the past year.

* Eighteen percent of high school students made a suicide plan during the past year.

* Female students and LGBQ+ students are experiencing alarming rates of violence, poor mental health, and suicidal thoughts and behaviors.

There are many reasons for this deterioration in mental health among young people. Examples include increased academic pressure, family issues, substance abuse, other addictions, sexual identity issues, lack of sleep, poverty, pregnancy, negative peer pressure, bullying, and violence.

Overuse of technology and social media has also been a critical factor when looking at the increase in teen mental health issues. Although social media has been helpful to some teens who need to feel more connected, it can also have a negative impact. For example, spending more than 3 hours a day on social media can be harmful to the mental well-being of young people (Haidt, 2024). According to a Gallup survey, the average amount of time teenagers in the United States spend on social media is 4.8 hours per day, which is having a significant negative impact on their mental health (Rothwell, 2023).

Too many of our youth are trying to cope with these issues alone, not knowing who they can turn to for help. There is an urgency for educators, especially school counselors and social workers, to be freed from many of their non-counseling tasks so they can become more available to address these increasing mental health concerns in students. According to the American School Counselor Association's (ASCA) Ethical Standards (2022), "School counselors have unique qualifications and skills to implement a comprehensive school counseling program." These standards also state that a counselor should "advocate for a school counseling program free of non-school-counseling assignments identified by the ASCA National Model: A Framework for School Counseling Programs," which was published by ASCA in 2019.

If school personnel are not following this national model and counselors and social workers are unable to reach these students who desperately need help, this can pose a serious problem that should be addressed by the administration. School district leaders should ensure that proper use of professional counselors is being tapped in all our schools. School counselors are in the schools to help students socially, emotionally, and academically. They are there to meet with students individually or in small groups, help in creating peer programs, and according to ASCA, "provide opportunities for all students to develop a positive attitude toward learning, effective learning strategies, self-management and social skills and an understanding that lifelong learning is part of long-term career success" (ASCA, 2022). With the current mental health crisis among our youth today, it is imperative that students have adequate access to and support from professional school counselors and other mental health caregivers such as social workers and psychologists.

Recommended Insights and Strategies

Learn what your school's policy is on how students should seek different kinds of help when needed.

- At the beginning of the year, ensure that all support staff are introduced to students and clearly explain to students how they can access their services. The support staff need to be available to effectively address or refer any mental health issues with students.

- Every student in the school should be able to identify at least one school professional who they can easily access for personal support when needed.

- In addition, students should be familiar with what support programs or groups exist and how to use them.

- School administrators should ensure that the guidelines from the professional organizations that represent your support staff are being followed.

Reaching Students Who Avoid Seeking Out Help From Others

So how do we get below the surface of a teen who is not willing to share how they really feel? It's not easy spending time with a defiant or depressed teen, but connection can be the very thing this young person needs at that moment. Sometimes it requires being creative in the way we ask questions. I have found that students can engage in conversation much better while being distracted in manipulating something with their hands, such as drawing, molding clay, or doing something together such as shooting baskets, taking a walk, listening to their favorite music, or playing their favorite game. This can place them at ease so they don't feel like they are being interrogated. Then ask a few *what* or *how* questions to start a conversation. Avoid questions that only require a *yes* or *no* answer (teens are too good at this). It is amazing how this strategy can make a difference in whether a student will feel comfortable in sharing their feelings with someone.

Tweens and teens are very good at pretending they are fine, so pay attention to their body language. Looking away or down when you ask them a question, crossing their arms, and fidgeting in their chair can all be signs that there is more going on under the surface. I know of a principal who said he made it a habit of asking some of his seniors the question, "Who are you?" toward the end of the school year. He mentioned asking one student, the valedictorian of his class, who was not able to answer and began to get very emotional. Sometimes the questions we ask can provide a springboard to deeper conversations. The important thing is to show you care and that you are at least trying.

Social media has become a popular place where lots of young people go to when they are feeling depressed or overwhelmed. They go online to seek out others who understand what they are going through. Up to 95% of teens between the ages of 13 and 17 say they use a social media platform, according to a report from U.S. Surgeon General Vivek Murthy. He warned that "social media use is a main contributor to depression, anxiety and other problems in the nation's teenagers" (Edwards & Jackson, 2023). This is very alarming to think many teens would rather go online to seek help from perfect strangers than to seek out help from an adult they know. This should motivate us even more to try to reach these young people who need our help.

Asking students where they see themselves in a year, five years, or as adults can help open up an entire conversation and provide a glimpse into how they actually feel about themselves. So, strive to ask the question (maybe several times in different ways). Don't be afraid to be direct with teens. They would rather you be open and genuine than avoiding the actual issue or problem. Once a teen begins sharing, it's important to *listen*! Don't make the mistake many do when talking to a teen—judging, advising, or talking about their own experience—just simply listen. Be patient, as some teens take a while to share their true emotions. The best listeners are those who don't interrupt, don't judge or react to what they are hearing, and reflect back what they heard using a summary of what was shared to show them how deeply they care. Listening can go a long way. It is something our world needs much more of.

Consider this famous quote by Stephen R. Covey: "Most people do not listen with the intent to understand; they listen with the intent to reply." Make sure you have the time and energy and can give this teen your full, undistracted attention. At school there is only so much time you can give. Perhaps meet with the student after school or at least let them know in advance how much time you do have to listen.

Some students often find themselves in trouble and are referred to a school administrator or the resource officer. They may not seek out help at school since they believe they are perceived by staff as the school troublemaker. The consequence for these students may be suspension or expulsion, which unfortunately is likely to end up with the student wanting to give up on school and eventually dropping out. Learn some strategies for how you can approach teens if you find they avoid approaching you. Creating an environment of caring and acceptance can help teens feel safe to seek out help when they need it. Peer programs are also a very effective way to do this since teens are more likely to talk with their peers about their personal problems. When adults can't be available for a student who urgently needs someone to talk to, it helps having trained peer listeners who can, especially if that teen has difficulty trusting adults.

Recommended Insights and Strategies

Evaluate Your School's Trainings on Dropout Prevention Issues

Rate how effective you believe your school is in offering trainings to staff and students in each of the following areas.

(Continued)

(Continued)

	EFFECTIVENESS			
	LOW	SOMEWHAT	HIGHLY	VERY HIGHLY
Bullying/ Cyberbullying				
Discouragement/ Depression				
Self-Injury				
Suicide Prevention				
Disconnectedness				
Oppositional Defiant Chronic Discipline Issues				
Stress/Anxiety				
Addiction/ Substance Abuse				
Peer Pressure				
Anger Management				
Gender Identity				
Gang Violence				
School Violence				
Social Media Addiction				
Impulsiveness/Self-Regulation				
Chronic Absenteeism				
Victims of Physical/ Emotional Abuse or Trauma				
Grief & Loss				
Other:				

- Identify staff in your school (or community) with expertise in the areas where training is needed and who could present an in-service training to staff, students, or both.

- Start a mental health club at your school. Involve other support staff to help get one started. There are several organizations that can help you:

Resources for Starting a Mental Health Club

NAMI (National Alliance on Mental Illness): www.nami.org

Broward County Mental Health Awareness Club: www.browardschools.com/Page/65647

Empowerment Clubs: www.erikaslighthouse.org

We Are Active Minds Clubs: www.activeminds.org/programs

- Learn to identify the red flags in student behavior. The Mayo Clinic provides a list of emotional and behavioral changes to look for in a teen who may be depressed. Learn to identify the red flags in student behavior to discern who could be either depressed and/or in need of help.

Emotional Changes

Be alert for emotional changes, such as:

- Feelings of sadness, which can include crying spells for no apparent reason

- Frustration or feelings of anger, even over small matters

- Feeling hopeless or empty

- Irritable or annoyed mood

- Loss of interest or pleasure in usual activities

- Loss of interest in, or conflict with, family and friends

- Low self-esteem

- Feelings of worthlessness or guilt

- Fixation on past failures or exaggerated self-blame or self-criticism

- Extreme sensitivity to rejection or failure, and the need for excessive reassurance

- Trouble thinking, concentrating, making decisions, and remembering things

- Ongoing sense that life and the future are grim and bleak

- Frequent thoughts of death, dying, or suicide

(Continued)

(Continued)

Behavioral Changes

Watch for changes in behavior, such as:

- Tiredness and loss of energy

- Insomnia or sleeping too much

- Changes in appetite, decreased appetite and weight loss, or increased cravings for food and weight gain

- Use of alcohol or drugs

- Agitation or restlessness, for example, pacing, handwringing, or an inability to sit still

- Slowed thinking, speaking, or body movements

- Frequent complaints of unexplained body aches and headaches, which may include frequent visits to the school nurse

- Social isolation

- Poor school performance or frequent absences from school

- Less attention to personal hygiene or appearance

- Angry outbursts, disruptive or risky behavior, or other acting-out behaviors

- Self-harm (for example, cutting or burning)

- Making a suicide plan or a suicide attempt

(Copied with permission from the Mayo Clinic, 2022)

Helping Students Find and Create Connection

According to a 2021 national survey by the CDC, "youth who feel connected at school are less likely to experience risks related to substance use, mental health, violence, and sexual behavior" (CDC, 2023b). Unless teens experience a strong connection to school or have something to look forward to there, it is very easy for them to find a connection elsewhere that could be harmful (Wilkins et al., 2023). For me, that connection was spending time with my boyfriend, who was a high school dropout. He encouraged me to skip school, so I was not motivated to find other interests at school. On the other hand, some teens can be encouraged positively by their peers to find things they enjoy about school. These students are able to explore clubs that match their interests, an athletic sport, or some other extracurricular activity. However, not all students are able to find something at school that interests them. If a student is not interested in sports, music, art, chess, or anything else the school offers, they may feel that school is just not for them. The answer for some students may be to create their own club or group. Creating a club or group likely needs to be approved by the leaders of that school. You can be the teacher or leader to help students facilitate this.

Let's face it, if school staff don't feel a connection to others in their school, how likely are they to continue wanting to go to work every day? In the same way, students need to feel a sense of connection and belonging. Tweens and teens are social beings and need in-person contact to feel validated and accepted.

Educators need to seek out those students who seem to be quiet or alone often or those in trouble often. Find out their interests and strengths and then encourage them to utilize their talent into something they can feel proud of. These students can make great leaders, and being in the position of role models to their peers can sometimes cause their behavior to improve. Whether it's tutoring a student, orientating a new student, or helping with a school-wide project, they can benefit from being involved and feeling valued, which can cause them to be more connected to their school community.

It's important to not be afraid to take a chance on allowing the student who causes trouble in class to help lead the class one day. Your quiet students who don't participate in class could help organize a class project. Every student is valuable and gifted in some way. They just need opportunities where they can experience feeling accepted and valuable.

Recommended Insights and Strategies

- Provide opportunities for those students who are less connected in school to be recognized by sharing their personal strengths and interests.

- Consider a teacher advisor, freshman focus, or similar program where teachers meet weekly with small groups of students throughout the year to discuss issues or concerns. These meetings can also be used for sharing opportunities to be more involved.

(Continued)

(Continued)

- Involve students who seem disconnected to be part of a peer program such as peer helping or peer mentoring. Students who are selected and trained to be peer helpers often benefit more than the peers they meet with to help. In addition, these students can sometimes reach out to those students who, like them, may feel alienated or disconnected in the school.

- Discuss in a staff meeting ideas for how your school can more effectively reach disconnected students.

Providing Restorative Discipline Practices

Between 1990 and the early 2000s, many schools handled discipline issues using a "zero-tolerance" approach, with punitive measures such as paddling (in some schools), suspensions, or expulsions for more serious offenses. This discipline practice was used mainly in the secondary schools. Then suspensions increased and racial disparities in student discipline practices also increased (Perera & Diliberti, 2023). The Learning Policy Institute states that years of data have shown that certain groups of students are disproportionately suspended, including students of color, students receiving special education services, students from low-income families, LGBTQ students, and males (Leung-Gagné et al., 2022).

Studies have also found that school suspensions may have a long-lasting negative impact on students who are suspended or expelled. Suspended students are less likely to graduate from high school and college, and they are more likely to be involved in the criminal justice system (Alvarez, 2021). Suspensions do not address the reasons for students' inappropriate behaviors and do not teach students more appropriate ways to handle these conflicts that caused the suspension. It's just a temporary Band-Aid on a much deeper wound.

Following the pandemic, there was a nation-wide surge in student discipline problems. Many students were expected to make the transition from a virtual platform to live school again while dealing with the social and emotional problems prompted by the pandemic. This transition caused some students to act out in an attempt to deal with their emotions (Clark, 2022).

Many schools now have in place alternative initiatives to deal with discipline issues. Some of these include school resource officers (SROs), in-school suspensions (ISSs) as an alternative to out-of-school suspensions, peer mediation, positive behavioral intervention and supports (PBIS), restorative justice programs, and multi-tiered systems of support (MTSS). These sound like great alternatives to a zero-tolerance approach practiced previously, except it's unclear how many schools are actually practicing them.

Let's look more closely at one of these practices: restorative justice. While strengthening the school climate, this approach encourages a supportive relationship with the student. It addresses the inappropriate behaviors by working with them to improve in-school relationships and teach skills such as self-regulation and healthy coping practices. What many of these young people need is helpful approaches to get to the underlying cause of the problem. Restorative practices are used as a tool to build community and relationships. This takes more time and commitment, which are the two things numerous school personnel say they don't have enough of. Although these approaches take time to implement, it will save the school time and headaches later. Restorative practices require stable leadership, routine meetings, trainings, and consistent follow-up and support (Goodwin, 2021). This is a much more effective method for working with teens at risk of dropping out.

Restorative circles and impromptu student conferences are two approaches of restorative practices. Restorative circles involve students meeting in a circle with a trained leader to take turns listening and sharing. Circles can be used for a wide range of purposes, such as building community, helping students connect their experiences to academic matter, or inviting a student back to school after an extended absence (Klevan, 2021). Impromptu student conferences involve a meeting between the student and teacher in an attempt for the teacher to check in with that student without disrupting class time. This can be a discussion outside the classroom to explore ways to redirect their behavior.

Recommended Insights and Strategies

- Implement restorative practices in your school.
  There are several organizations that can provide this training.
  www.restorativesolutions.us/schools/restorative-training-modules;
  www.nationalcenterforrestorativejustice.com/education
  https://conflictcenter.org/programs-training/schools/restorative-practices-program/

(Continued)

(Continued)

- Know the people in your school who are in charge of restorative practices.

- Discuss your school's discipline protocol and how restorative practices are being used. Are these practices working? If not, how can they be improved?

- Provide step-by-step strategies for teachers in how to have a positive interaction with a misbehaving student in the classroom. For example, see the responsibility-centered discipline approach: https://www.givemfive.com.

- What type of student discipline problems could benefit from a restorative approach rather than suspension or expulsion?

Developing and Enhancing a Personal Support System

Not all students who are deeply troubled or facing a crisis will choose to go to the counseling office. Instead, they may engage in an altercation with a staff member or another student or make a scene in class, which would result in being sent to the principal's office for disciplinary action. Sometimes the principal would refer the student to the counseling office. Teens often feel their situation is hopeless and act out impulsively, not knowing what else to do. If they are not aware of what the school counselors can provide, they will take matters in their own hands.

When you ask these teens, "Who can you talk to when you are having problems?" many will say their friends. They have many reasons for not seeking help from adults; *I don't want to be a burden, they will judge me, they will tell my parents, they will think I'm crazy, they won't understand.* It helps for students to be informed at the beginning of the year who they can go to if they need help. If a school counselor is not available at the time a student is in crisis, then the school should have a list of others who would be able to help, for example, a school social worker, school psychologist, behavioral specialist, intervention specialist, or peer listener. Teens need to know that there are adults available at school who can provide support and with whom they can trust.

Social media has become a "safe haven" for many students experiencing personal problems. According to the Pew Research Center, many teens say social media makes them feel like they have people who can support them when going through tough times (Anderson et al., 2022).

It is unfortunate that some young people will choose to avoid speaking about personal issues with a professional counselor. Instead, they rely on social media as their exclusive resource.

Here are several ways schools can provide a support system to our students who require more social or emotional help.

Small Support and Counseling Groups

I wish I could have participated in a small support group when I was in middle school. It could have helped to have a safe place to share and discuss with other students some of the issues I was experiencing in my life. Small support groups did not exist in my school, but years later ASCA included Group Work in their ethical standards. School counselors are trained in conducting small groups, which can include students who are at risk of dropping out. As a former school counselor, I made sure I provided groups to my at-risk students even though I had a principal who did not understand this part of the role of the professional school counselor. I decided the only way to effectively reach some students was to involve them in a group where they could safely talk about their life challenges.

In 2015, the Missouri Department of Elementary and Secondary Education and the Missouri Center for Career Education developed the Missouri Comprehensive Guidance and Counseling Program, referred to as the "Missouri Model." Not only does it provide support for having small groups in the school, but it also provides step-by-step guidelines for counselors in how to implement and run these groups. Since then, other states have provided guidelines for small groups based on this model but with modifications for today's trends. Group counseling can help reduce social isolation and undesirable emotions, as well as increase positive peer relations and a sense of belonging (ASCA, 2024). Students benefit from not feeling alone in their situation and having the support of others. All age levels can benefit from small groups.

A High School Anger Management Group

At my school I started an anger management group for students who were having trouble with anger issues and sometimes acting out their anger at school. After discovering this commonality among several students who often came to the counseling office, I decided to bring them together in a group. Most of these teens had one or both parents experiencing substance abuse problems or domestic violence in the home. These students had not learned enough appropriate ways to understand and deal with their anger. The group met in my counseling office, and we would spend time sharing issues of the week but also work on appropriate ways for them to handle their anger and learn better coping skills. Role playing these skills was extremely helpful to them. Just giving these students a safe place to vent once a week helped them to share their feelings and learn other ways to express their emotions toward their classmates or teachers. The important thing was that they felt heard and accepted and sensed that someone actually cared.

A Teen Pregnancy Group

At my school we had at least four girls who were already moms and a few more who were expecting. I decided to start a teen pregnancy support group, meeting during lunch since that was an important time for them to keep healthy by eating well. I was able to arrange their schedules so they all shared the same lunch period. It gave us enough time to practice some basic parenting skills and share some of their concerns. I would sometimes play calming music and have them all practice relaxation skills. I think that time together helped them to encourage and support one another and learn about what to expect from the ones who were already moms. We also had a field trip to a local hospital's maternity ward to walk through what to expect when they were actually in labor. This helped them to better prepare and helped diminish many of the fears they had about giving birth.

A few of the teen moms were trained in peer leadership skills and spoke at the middle school to groups of students, usually during physical education class. They gave such a realistic picture of what life was like being a teen parent that several became very emotional when talking to the group. Once when there were a few male hecklers in the group, one of the girls confronted them by telling them, "Laugh now but you won't be laughing when you have to support your child until they're eighteen." Before our last group meeting, we had the moms bring their babies into a carpeted room and practice learning how to give infant massages. It was a very meaningful and impactful group for these girls.

Here is a list of other small support groups that could be led at your school depending on the student needs and available time.

- Self-regulation

- Self-esteem/self-confidence

- Social issues with boys/girls

- Grief and loss

- Mental health issues

- Decision-making and conflict management

- Bullying

- Stress and anxiety

- Discouragement and disconnection

- Gender identity issues

- Peers in crisis

Tips for setting up and leading a small group:

- Find a common issue with the students you see on a regular basis, or conduct a student needs assessment to discover what issues are of the most concern.

- Inform your principal about the group, providing the results of the needs assessment.

- Decide if you want to conduct a facilitated group (leader follows the issues expressed during sessions) or conduct a curriculum-based group (leader follows a planned out, more structured, activity-based group).

- Obtain permission from the parents/guardians of students wanting to join the group.

- A group size of five to eight students is ideal.

- Meet at least one session per week for 6 to 12 weeks.

- Meet during lunch, exploratory period, after school, etc.

- A duration of 30 to 50 minutes per session works well.

Resources for Leading a Small Group for Teens

Available from YouthLight:

Get Your Group On! Volumes 1 & 2

Salvaging Sisterhood

ACTivities for Group Work With Adolescents

Black Girl Blues

Thrive in the Hive

Girls in the Lead

Available from Boys Town Press:

Everyone's Talking

Teaching Social Skills to Youth

Building Resiliency in Teens

Teens Social Skills Strategy

Available from Whole Person Associates, Inc.:

Teens: Managing Life's Expectations

Teen Resiliency-Building Workbook

Wellness Activities for Youth

Student Peer Helping and Mentoring

Another way to provide more support for students is by utilizing positive peer support. I am a firm believer in students being trained in how to reach out as helpers to their peers. ASCA also supports Student Peer-Support Programs and provides guidelines in their ethical standards for school counselors. When students are systematically trained in helping skills such as listening, encouraging, decision-making, mediation, and referral protocol, they will benefit themselves as much, if not more than the students with whom they will be helping (Varenhorst, 1992). Several of my peer helpers told me years later how much the program helped them beyond high school into their adult lives.

I have experienced firsthand the power of peer mentoring. When I was a single teen mom, I had a mentor who wasn't formally trained, but she encouraged me to earn my GED and then continue my education. Without her help I am not sure I would have achieved my two college degrees. I will always remember how impactful it was to have someone who believed in my potential when I did not. She encouraged me to recognize my personal strengths and inspired me to develop and follow a plan to improve my life.

Was there a mentor or peer support person who encouraged you at a tough time in your life? Reflect back to what qualities made that person so effective. These are the same characteristics you should look for in selecting and training student peer helpers. It's very important when selecting potential helpers or mentors that they represent the diversity of your student population. Whether they are going to mentor younger students or be peer helpers for students near their age, there are some basic steps that are needed. I started peer programs at the elementary, middle, and high school levels, including my work with juvenile offenders. Many students can become impactful peer helpers with the proper training.

Training

You must take into consideration the age of your students. In middle school, I trained a group of eight eighth-graders once a week. At the high school level, since I wanted to have a larger group of helpers, I trained twelve seniors, with a few assigned as mentors for ninth-graders. I conducted an entire weekend of training with these students. To do this, you need to locate a facility that can accommodate students with appropriate housing and adequate supervision. In my experience, having an entire weekend to conduct training allowed for a more in-depth preparation that offers ample time for students to role-play advanced listening and helping skills. But it is also possible to train peer helpers in weekly sessions at school.

Student peer helpers can help to decrease the number of "frequent flyers" coming to the counseling office and can also provide a helpful outreach to students who would benefit by having someone who is a good listener and encourager.

Here are some things to consider when implementing a peer program at your school.

Tips for setting up and leading an effective peer helper or peer mentoring/tutoring program for students who are at risk of dropping out of school:

- Find one or two staff members who are interested and committed to helping you.

- Decide on how large you want the student helper group to be (it's okay to start small with 6–8 students)

- Select student helpers who reflect the diversity and the needs of the population to be served (these students can be referred by teachers and other staff).

- Decide on when and how often students are able to meet for training and then serve as helpers.

Tips for training the student peer helpers and mentors:

- Decide where and when peers will meet with students.

- Provide an overview of what they will be doing after training.

- Practice asking open-ended questions like "What?" and "How?" versus close-ended and "Why?" questions.

- Practice active listening and feeling-focused responding skills, which summarize what a person said using a word that represents what that person might be feeling.

- Pair students up and allow time for students to role-play listening skills.

- Discuss confidentiality. Anything told to peer helpers by the students they are helping must be kept just between them and not shared with anyone else unless there is danger to self or others.

- Discuss limitations that peer helpers have in dealing with more serious issues that may come up and how and when to refer a student to an adult leader or adult helper at the school.

Resources for Peer Helper/Mentor Training

Meaningful Mentoring (YouthLight)

Helping Adolescents Know What to Do When a Peer Is in Crisis (YouthLight)

Training Peer Helpers: Coaching Youth to Communicate, Solve Problems, and Make Decisions (YouthLight)

Jennifer Claire Moore Foundation, https://jennifermoor-efoundation.com/pages/peerhelpers-program

National Association of Peer Program Professionals, https://peerprogramprofessionals.org

Home Visits

Growing up, my mom had little support of any kind while raising seven children and caring for my dad who had a mental illness. She was also dealing with a daughter (me) who kept getting into trouble and running away. A home visit could have provided a counselor, social worker, or other caregiver the needed insight into what our family was dealing with. Home visits can help encourage a positive partnership between the school personnel and the parents or guardians. If a home visit isn't possible, school personnel should at least try to meet parents or guardians of students whenever and however they can. In these meetings, be sure to be encouraging about them and their child. Include some open-ended questions, inviting them to share their perspectives and listen attentively and patiently to their answers. Remember that one of the most important goals of the meeting is to try to nurture a mutual partnership between you and the parents or guardians, with the ultimate intention of helping their child.

Ironically, my first school job was as a dropout prevention counselor at a small rural middle school. I understood where many of these students were coming from because I was once where they were. In this program I was encouraged to go on home visits, which sometimes meant waking kids up in their homes and driving them to school or going to their usual hangouts and trying to convince them to return to school. When I went to their homes, I was able to see first-hand their situations and that sometimes gave me ideas about how I could help them. During many of these visits, I was also able to help the parents by referring them to agencies where they could find assistance with their situation. Home visits were an important part of establishing a connection with many struggling parents and their children.

Later, when I was a high school counselor, I was not able to visit all my students' parents or guardians, but I tried to visit those whose teen was at higher risk of dropping out. It really helped to understand where these students were coming from so that I could better provide services for them and their parents. I also met with the parents of my peer helpers and mentors, so they knew who I was and what their child was training to do. These parents were all very supportive when they learned that their child would be a peer leader at school.

Recommended Insights and Strategies

- School principals must understand and ensure that their school counselors adhere to the professional standards set forth by the American School Counselor Association (ASCA, 2022). It's critical, for example, that counselors are able to devote much of their time directly helping students and not be bogged down with clerical, substitute teaching, and quasi-administrative tasks such as test monitoring and bus or lunch duties. Of course, school counselors, like other staff, can be expected to take on some non-counseling initiatives, but they should spend most of their time utilizing their professional expertise by working directly with students and their parents/guardians and teachers. When school counselors are encouraged (and expected) to do this, they can provide invaluable help to many more students, including those who are at risk of dropping out of school.

- Counselors should plan to make some periodic home visits and, if possible, include the school social worker or other support staff from the school.

- If a home visit isn't possible, try to find another way to contact parents of students who are experiencing difficulties at school. Perhaps you can plan to meet parents at a game, school-wide event, or other activity.

- Know the professionals at your school or in the community who are available to meet with students who are struggling with mental health issues. They might be able to help reach parents you are not able to.

- At the beginning of the school year, school personnel should provide parents with a list of names and contact information for the different services the school and community provide.

- Plan a fun night at school where you can have food and provide a casual drop-in experience for parents. This can be a positive way to help parents feel invited in a less intimidating setting.

Encouraging Personal Strengths and Purpose

Many teens (and adults for that matter) can't tell you what their life's purpose is. They may appear to have a great life and have much going for them, yet they actually feel the opposite about their life. Unfortunately, we all know of students who were successful athletes, popular with peers, gifted academically, or involved in several leadership roles or clubs but then took their own life. We are left baffled, trying to make sense of how they could become so deeply discouraged that they would undertake a permanent end to their lives.

When working with youth, especially at a juvenile prison, I noticed many of them lacked feelings of self-worth and self-confidence. Few of them could describe any positive purpose they had for their lives. It's difficult to discover a positive life purpose without first believing that your life has value and potential. We can help students discover their life purpose by first helping them explore their personal strengths and how they can continuously tap these strengths as they encounter life's challenges.

There was an especially helpful activity I used with the incarcerated males I worked with. I asked them to write out four or five of their personal strengths. They often sat there staring at the paper unable to write down even one. They explained that they really had not thought about this since they saw themselves as juvenile offenders and were labeled as troublemakers or delinquents most of their life. I would instruct them to take a deeper look into the challenges they had experienced in their lives and how they overcame them. Many had experienced more trauma at a young age than most adults have in their entire lifetime. I asked them to think of what they did to overcome each of these challenges and presented them with a list of personal strength words to look over (see the list later in this chapter). I wanted to start them thinking about what strengths they used that helped them survive.

This was probably the first time these juveniles had ever thought about having positive strengths rather than focusing on their weaknesses or getting into trouble. It was a struggle for them to come up with just three strength words. But once they realized these were strengths they already had, they were able to explore different ways they could tap their unique combination of strengths when facing other challenges in their life.

I also trained a few of these juveniles to be peer leaders to the young people just arriving at the facility so they could help them with the transition. This allowed them to be in the role of a helper and leader instead of a juvenile delinquent. They enjoyed participating and started to finally find a new sense of life purpose. Not all incarcerated students believed they could change or become something other than a criminal. But for those who desired to live a different life and wanted to make something of themselves, discovering their personal strengths was a powerful first step.

One of the most important personal strengths that could be especially helpful to potential school dropouts is resourcefulness. Resourcefulness involves knowing where, when, and how to seek help from sources other than from oneself. Too often, these students don't fully realize how helpful others' suggestions, insights, and supportive caring can be. And in many cases, they don't seek others' help. Encourage these students to brainstorm with you where they could go to for help in various situations. Sometimes, they may need assistance in seeking help. They might need someone to actually refer and accompany them to a meeting with someone who could help.

Two other important personal strengths for these young people to have and grow are grit and resiliency. It is not necessary to experience a profoundly difficult situation to have grit and resiliency. Young people can be encouraged to be aware of and use these strengths when facing many small obstacles. Encourage these students to persevere in situations when they are otherwise easily discouraged. Help them to discover how their struggling and failing can help make them stronger.

Many people can help instill these personal strengths, including parents/guardians, grandparents, school staff, peers, mentors, and other family or community members who are there when an opportunity for personal encouragement presents itself. Sometimes just one person can teach a student about their personal strengths and purpose in life and ultimately help them turn their entire life around.

Recommended Insights and Strategies

- Encourage students to develop and describe realistic short-term goals and how they can start working toward each of them. Examples include to achieve a passing grade on a math test, to get along better with a particularly challenging teacher, to ask for help with a problem with a friend, or make more and better friends.

- Help students list some steps toward achieving their life purpose. These can be short term and/or long term.

- Identify and encourage students' personal strengths. They can be reminded of these and use them in their self-talk when they work to deal with a challenge or difficult task. Utilize the Personal Strength Words list that follows to have students select three to five words that best describe their unique combination of personal strengths.

PERSONAL STRENGTH WORDS

Adventurous	Fair	Optimistic
Anger-Control Appreciative	Faithful	Organized
Artistic	Flexible	Patient
Athletic	Forgiving	Prepared
Brave	Generous	Punctual
Calm	Good-Sport	Reasonable
Caring	Hard-Worker	Resourceful
Cautious	Helpful	Respectful
Confident	Honest	Self-Aware
Considerate	Humble	Sensitive
Cooperative	Humorous	Supportive
Curious	Independent	Sharing
Dedicated	Insightful	Sincere
Dependable	Kind	Survivalist
Determined	Leader	Team-Player
Disciplined	Likable	Thoughtful
Encouraging	Motivated	Tolerant
Enthusiastic	Neat	Trustworthy
Friendly	Open-Minded	Unselfish

(Reprinted with permission from R. P. Bowman, 2024)

- Have students look for opportunities where they can strengthen their resourcefulness and grit by using their personal strengths. For example, work with them to brainstorm possible solutions to a challenge such as surviving a classroom they don't like or confronting someone who has been bothering them. Practice being more assertive.

Starting Early Is Best

A review of the literature on interventions designed to prevent students from dropping out shows that there are multiple risk factors that need to be addressed early in life rather than just in high schools (Lee-St. John et al., 2018; Long, 2017).

Middle and high school personnel have attempted to tackle the dropout problem for decades. This becomes more challenging by the time students reach high school. Many of the students I worked with at our state's juvenile prison said their problems started when they were in elementary school, and it went downhill from there. Most of them lacked classroom and family structure, supervision, and academic help starting at a young age. Reading was another significant factor; many incarcerated youths were reading at third- and fourth-grade levels. This correlation between students with low reading proficiency and increased chances of dropping out of school is not a new concern (Daniel et al., 2006; Glazer, 1978; Sparks, 2011, 2021). It appears that our nation's education decision-makers need to continue to make reading proficiency a high priority at all grade levels.

It is critical to intervene early because children who start underachieving in grade school are at higher risk of dropping out later. For example, students who repeat a grade in elementary school have been shown to be more likely than their peers to eventually drop out of high school (Giano et al., 2022). Many underperformers become stuck in a destructive mindset and give up trying. It's important for these students to practice skills in how to change this belief to a more positive and encouraging mindset. Parents, regardless of their education levels, need to partner with school personnel to encourage their children to believe in their personal value and potential. They should ensure there are continual opportunities in which children can feel successful as a result of their effort and determination.

Parents and guardians who dropped out themselves might have some negative recollections about their experiences as a young student in school. Patiently encourage them to work as closely as they can with their child on their schoolwork. Single parents can also feel especially uncomfortable when their children have difficulty in school. Some of these parents can easily become defensive because they feel they are ultimately responsible for difficulties in their child. As educators, we need to be sensitive toward and encourage these parents and always find a way to provide some positive news to them about their child. Even if that child is constantly acting out and getting into trouble, there is always something constructive that can be pointed out. For example, point out some personal strength words that describe their child. Then brainstorm with them how they could work with school personnel to help their child build on and improve their use of these strengths.

Educators need to provide opportunities for even our youngest students to share about their interests, joys, and concerns. Also, preschool and elementary schools need to set the stage for children to learn social and emotional insights and skills to help them build a strong foundation for success in school and life.

It's natural that some students are going to be more enjoyable for teachers to work with than others. However, it is critical to realize that some of the students with the most challenging attitudes and behaviors could become the most successful people later in life. Staying positive and encouraging with some of these students will require extraordinary patience. It's critical that school personnel, regardless of how frustrated they become with a student's behavior and/or attitude, retain a supportive belief that this student has value and potential and that they are cared about. This encouraging message can have a profound impact on a young person who might otherwise believe that others see them merely as annoying. An example of the impact that this encouraging attitude can have on a child can be found in the story " The Old Leather Jacket," included in Appendix E of this book.

Recommended Insights and Strategies

- Focus on students' personal strengths in all grades, and especially in the earlier years. Provide opportunities for students to be reminded of and use these strengths continually.

- Consider screening students in the school to determine those who demonstrate some risk factors for eventually dropping out of school. See *Screening Tool to Identify Students at Higher Risk for Dropping Out* in Appendix A of this book. This should be administered to all students in the school.

- Learn what programs your school district provides to help struggling students at the elementary level. Peer helping? Mentoring? After-school programs?

(Continued)

(Continued)

- Find ways for the middle and high school personnel and students to work more closely with the elementary schools in dropout prevention initiatives.

- Provide opportunities for young students to learn from their mistakes and grow their grit and resiliency. They can also learn about these strengths from stories of famous people who endured hardship and failure only to recover and eventually achieve great success. See Appendix C for a list.

- Encourage children to explore what lessons they can learn from disappointments. They can do this by brainstorming fresh ideas they could try in their next attempt to deal with the situation.

- Learn how you can better engage parents and guardians in helping their child become more successful in school. School staff can tap ideas from their colleagues who have success in engaging with parents. Likewise, parents can be encouraged to use ideas from other parents. A parent support group can provide valuable opportunities for parents to share and learn from one another.

Remembering It's Never Too Late

Every human being has the capability of achieving amazing things in their life. Teens just need to visualize a clear image of themselves as being successful and practice affirming self-talk to help them develop a more positive mindset about themselves and their potential. Believing in themselves is an important part of pursuing their educational and personal goals. It's important to help students practice imagining and talking to themselves about finishing school or passing their GED or going to college or working for that dream job they always wanted. These visualizations and self-conversations can boost their self-confidence, which they need to counter when frustration or discouragement start to set in.

I never imagined that I could go from dropping out of eighth grade and attending one week of high school to eventually earning a graduate degree from a university. The only way I could have achieved this was with lots of determination and persistence and with the help of others who encouraged and believed in me. One person in particular saw my potential and helped me to finally see it as well. Once I received my GED, it was another spark that lit the fire inside me. I finally had the drive to never give up!

In my work with students, I never liked hearing the statement "I can't . . ." I found the following reframing technique (Rex et al., 2022) to be very helpful to students who say this, especially if they are thinking of giving up. Encourage them to first change their "I can't . . ." to "I won't . . ." This will alert them to take responsibility and that this is their choice. Next, have them change the statement to "I will . . ." This reframing of their statement can help them change their mindset and commit to doing something to help them move forward. Just like in some of the stories I shared earlier, someone can help a potential school dropout to change their mindset and, by doing that, have a lifelong positive impact on their life.

All students need to dare to dream big. Students who are already failing in school often feel it's too late for them. It's difficult for many troubled youth to see themselves as anything other than a failure or disappointment to others. They tend to have a fixed mindset because they rarely or never experienced a positive outcome at school or in their personal life. This is especially true with teens who have been expelled or incarcerated.

For example, when I worked with a group of boys from the juvenile prison on life skills and employability skills; it opened up a whole new view of their future. This group met weekly for eight weeks. I made it clear to the boys that they would be treated with respect as long as they showed respect in return. As an incentive to complete the entire eight weeks, I told them they would receive a certificate of completion and I would take a professional photo of each of them wearing a dress shirt and tie. The only photos taken of them since their incarceration were of them wearing a jumpsuit with a number printed on it. They were very excited to have a professional-looking photo that they could share with their family. Perhaps more important, each of them would be able to see and show to their family an image of themselves as sharp-dressed, successful young men.

Peer Support

Positive peer influence is another way to keep some students from dropping out of school. The quality of the relationship a student develops with their best friend at school could play an important role in developing the right kind of motivation to complete the work required to earn a high school diploma (Véronneau & Trempe, 2024).

If you haven't already, read the inspiring story of the three troubled teens who frequently had trouble with the law and decided one day to make a pact to ensure they all graduated from high school. They later wrote the book *The Pact*, which describes how the three of them made a sworn promise to one another that they would each graduate from high school. Though there were some challenges they had to overcome along the way, all three honored their commitment to one another and eventually each earned doctorate degrees.

I was so moved by their story that I provided copies of the youth version they wrote, *We Beat the Street: How a Friendship Pact Led to Success*, to boys at the juvenile prison. I wanted them to see what can happen when you have peers who will encourage you and hold you accountable. Many of their former friends were a negative influence and led them into trouble and breaking the law. Making a pact together can help troubled teens provide mutual support and encouragement to one another that can help motivate them to persevere when facing challenges.

There are many benefits to implementing peer helper programs in schools. They can be especially helpful for students who might feel it's too late for them to ever graduate. Peer programs became popular during the 1970s. Schools found that peers who were high risk themselves benefited greatly by being a helper to others and were more likely to make better decisions while in the role of a peer helper (Varenhorst, 1992). When peer learning strategies are implemented in the classroom, teachers are more likely to observe higher levels of student functioning, fulfillment, and overall engagement. Peer helping programs can provide the support students need to continue in school even while living homeless, being a victim of bullying, having failing grades, or encountering other setbacks. Troubled teens especially need to experience connection and encouragement from their peers; for some, it may be the first time in their lives they ever felt this kind of support.

All schools should have some kind of a peer support program. These peers can be trained in how to see the warning signs of a student who is at risk of dropping out or may have other issues that could result in them becoming depressed or even suicidal. Peers are usually the first to know when another student is experiencing some kind of distress. With proper training, these peers can learn what to say and do in these situations and who to go to for help when it's a serious issue that requires adult intervention. I provide a school-based training for this kind of intervention in my book *Helping Adolescents Know What to Do When a Peer Is in Crisis*, published by YouthLight (S. Bowman, 2021). Peer helpers/mentors can also help at the college level to support first-year students acclimating to college life since many have a difficult time adjusting and sometimes drop out of college.

There are stories of students who dropped out of school but were able to find a job that didn't require a diploma or GED. These young adults may find success in life, but they will likely need to work harder at advancing in their job or career. There are also stories of successful adults who established a career without earning a diploma or GED, but that path likely included increased and deeper challenges they had to face and overcome.

Almost everyone has experienced challenges in life. More professionals need to share their personal testimonies of overcoming difficulties with their students, when appropriate. Whether you are a teacher, school counselor, social worker, administrator, or other school staff, if you can share your life experiences with a student at your school who is struggling you may be able to encourage them to not give up. At the same time, you don't have to be a former dropout or have experienced the same things your students are experiencing to be impactful. Imagine if they do the same for someone else and that person then touches the life of another—just think of the many whose lives will be forever changed.

I believe it is never too late to go back to school—just like Vivian Fahr from Louisiana didn't think it was too late when she received her GED at 88 years old! After dropping out of school to get married, years later she said she regretted never getting her high school diploma, so she decided to finally take her GED. Many need to hear the message to not let anyone tell you that it's too late or you're too old to continue your education! Or hear the words of Vivian Fahr: "If you want to do it and you put in the work and you make your mind up, you can do it" (Miller, 2021).

My Personal Story

After experiencing homelessness and emotional and physical abuse, I finally divorced Kevin when I was 19 and pregnant with my third child. Shortly after the divorce I met Iliana, who would change the trajectory of my life. Although she wasn't a part of any formal mentoring program, she worked in social services and decided to help me. I did not own a car, so she drove me and my girls to appointments, stores, and other places we needed to go. During our time together she would encourage me and tell me how much potential I had. She was the one responsible for making me consider college. With her help, I had a tutor come to my apartment twice a week to prepare me to take the GED

(Continued)

(Continued)

exam. This was very difficult for me since I had barely completed eighth grade and never really attended high school long enough to have learned anything. Now here I was with three children to raise and studying to take the high school equivalency exam. Although this diploma would not be equivalent to a four-year high school diploma, I felt it was my first step to feeling like I could succeed at something other than being a teen parent. After weeks of tutoring, I finally took my test but didn't pass all the parts. After several attempts, I eventually passed all of it. This was not easy, but I was determined and finally received my GED certificate! I was very proud of my achievement. It opened doors that I never dreamed could be opened by me.

Iliana was now encouraging me to apply to take classes at the local university. I had no idea how to do this since as a child, growing up with parents who had little formal education, I thought that only kids who were from wealthy families attended college. I needed to have more confidence in myself. I was never encouraged as a teen to think of going to college, but now with some assurance in my abilities from Iliana, I decided to try a few college courses.

After assistance completing all the paperwork in my application, I received the official acceptance letter from the University of Maine. This was extremely exciting and affirming to me. In addition to taking two credited classes, I was required to take four non-credit basic level courses. I had to find neighbors to watch my children while I attended school and find rides to my college classes. Although difficult, it was also a big step in moving forward in my life. I walked into my first class in a huge auditorium with a room full of students about my age. It was intimidating but exciting at the same time. I took diligent notes during class and soaked in everything I was exposed to. I had never felt this enthusiasm when I attended school as a child. It was the belief in myself that I could achieve something that made the difference. I now had a different mindset and a determination that one day I would graduate from college with a degree.

Having a mentor who helped me see the potential that I didn't know was there was essential in my personal growth. I needed that nudge to help me get jump-started. I had to face many challenges that other students in my classes didn't have to overcome. After my classes I would come home to a baby and two toddlers who really needed me. I had to juggle being a mom and a college student while surviving only on money I received from welfare, which was never enough to make ends meet. I eventually completed two college courses and was proving to myself that it's never too late!

Recommended Insights and Strategies

- Consider starting a peer and/or mentoring program to encourage students who are at risk of dropping out. Training and resources on this are included in the Developing and Enhancing a Personal Support System section.

- Consider having graduation coaches to help students work toward graduation. Discuss who could be good candidates.

- Provide opportunities for students to hear or read inspiring stories about students who overcame challenges before or after dropping out of school.

- Explore how your school can develop or enhance initiatives with its community to inspire young people to continue their education (e.g., new incentives, job shadowing, or internship opportunities).

Nine Strategies to Strengthen Dropout Prevention

6

Where do we go next? Tapping my own background, the experiences of others who have dropped out, and the research in dropout prevention, I have developed the following list of recommended strategies. Successful dropout prevention takes a combination of efforts at the community, school, classroom, and individual student levels to have a substantial impact.

1. **Create a dropout prevention team.** This team should meet periodically and consist of a school administrator, a member of staff such as a teacher or school counselor, parents/guardians, a community representative, and a student, if possible. Start the team as early as possible in the school year. The National Dropout Prevention Center can be a particularly valuable resource for this team through its guidelines and recommendations. (https://drop outprevention.org/effective-strategies)

2. **Continually seek out students who seem disconnected and create connections.** Meet with staff and/or parents regularly to develop ideas and initiatives to help potential dropout students become more engaged with someone or something in school. Determine first if these students' basic needs are being met. Many students come to school hungry, and they may seem disinterested because they can't concentrate on an empty stomach. Conduct a survey using the *Screening Tool to Identify Students at Higher Risk for Dropping Out* in Appendix A to recognize students who are most at risk of dropping out. Assign at least one staff member, mentor, or peer helper to work with each student individually and identify the student's needs, interests, and personal strengths. Every student who is at risk for dropping

out should be able to identify at least one person in the school with whom they feel a supportive connection.

3. **Implement a comprehensive student-peer support program.** By implementing a peer support program (peer listeners, mental health club, student mentors), you are providing more opportunities for your students at risk to develop a supportive relationship. When selecting students for this program, be sure to include some students who would not ordinarily be selected by school staff as "model" students. Sometimes the best peer helpers are those who have experienced alienation or school discipline issues themselves. They may be able to connect with others more effectively since they can identify with them. Recommendations on how to set up a skills-based peer support program can be found in *Meaningful Mentoring: A Handbook of Effective Strategies, Projects and Activities* (R. P. Bowman & Bowman, 2019) and in *Helping Adolescents Know What to Do When a Peer Is in Crisis* (S. Bowman, 2021), published through YouthLight.

4. **Provide more support programs to address the unique needs some students may have.** Increase the connections between students at risk and your school's social workers, counselors, and other mental health support staff. Students need to know that there are adult professionals available at school to help them. Create easy and inviting ways students can access these supports when needed. Ensure that parents are made aware of what mental health services are offered in the school. Also explain that these school personnel are there to help them as well as their child. Make available small support groups for students at risk for dropping out. Also, consider setting up a mental health club for students in the school.

5. **Be sure your administration supports and implements some social/emotional learning (SEL) in all classrooms.** Have a school-wide, student interactive approach to teaching SEL in the classrooms. SEL skills are critically needed to help provide a solid foundation for their learning. There are many programs available online that offer programs and recommendations.

6. **Encourage students to discover their sense of belonging, personal strengths, and life purpose.** Everyone has a deep need to feel a sense of belonging. There is a strong connection between a student's sense of belonging and a positive self-esteem. A feeling of belonging in school is built from positive connections

with peers, school staff, programs, and groups. It is also built from at least some sense of academic success (Edwards, 1995). Whenever possible, help encourage students to strengthen their positive connections in the school with students, adults, and programs.

It is also helpful for students to be able to identify and name their personal strengths. Show them a list of personal strength words (see list in Chapter 5) and ask them to choose which ones best describe them. It can help students to recall their strengths and use them if and when they become discouraged. Students should also think about and be able to verbalize their life's purpose, which can be challenging, but taking time to explore examples of different purposes people have in their lives can help students select one or more to describe their own.

7. **Provide opportunities for all staff to be encouraged and supported.** Schools need to create a safe and supportive environment for everyone. Be sure to include opportunities for staff to share concerns and ideas with one another. Regularly include encouragement and opportunities for staff to support one another. Collegial support among staff will help to create a more positive school climate. An excellent resource that provides opportunities for this is *1-Minute Encouragers for Educators* (Fikac & Bowman, 2024).

8. **Include a restorative approach for dealing with student discipline problems.**
    All schools need to practice a restorative approach to student discipline. This will improve the climate and culture of the school and send the message to students that the school cares about them. This caring attitude can go a long way for a student who does not have positive role models in their life or adults who they can trust. A supportive relationship with students will create an environment that is more inviting and accepting. There are many suggestions for restorative practices available online. Make sure you are aware of alternative programs in your area that may be a better fit for students who struggle consistently. Learn about programs that can also help support the parents of these youth and inform parents about them.

9. **Provide a variety of after-school opportunities to strengthen their desire to learn.**
    Many students can benefit from after-school programs that offer reading initiatives, homework help, hobbies, or physical outlets. After-school programs are crucial dropout prevention initiatives,

especially in communities that are lacking in activities or alternatives for youth. Sometimes after-school programs offer transportation for the students. If communities do not provide positive opportunities for these students, they will find other activities that are not so positive, like experimenting with drugs and alcohol or other high-risk behaviors. Be sure school support staff are made aware of all the local community-based programs so they can share them with students and their parents.

Assess your school and rate its effectiveness in implementing each of these nine suggestions on a scale of 1 to 5 (5 being very strong and 1 being very weak or nonexistent). Use this assessment as a basis for setting fresh goals for your school's dropout prevention initiative. If you determine that there are just too many of these items to realistically address adequately, don't stop there. Determine which of these recommendations could be implemented or strengthened first and make this a wake-up call to take your gains where you can get them.

Increasing Parent/ Guardian Involvement

7

Parents and other caregivers have a huge influence on their children's success in school. If they have a negative attitude toward the school, its personnel, or schooling in general this will likely have a negative impact on their child's motivation to succeed. School personnel should proactively work to connect with parents to help change this attitude. Parents need to feel like they are part of their child's success. Parent involvement in their child's school and education has many positive benefits. It has been shown to help improve kids' behavior, grades, and social skills and increase their chances of graduating (Henderson & Mapp, 2022). Valuing parents' efforts and inviting parents to help work alongside the school on behalf of their child can encourage them to be more involved with their child's education. Increased communication between parents and school staff will ensure that these meetings are inviting and encouraging.

Providing timely and encouraging information to parents is critical, but too much advice can quickly turn off a parent's motivation to keep listening, especially if it makes them feel criticized or guilty. While parents can benefit from some tips and suggestions, school personnel must be cautious how this information is conveyed. Another way to provide this information to parents is through parent support groups. These groups provide an empathetic approach and assure participants that they are not alone with their issues. There are likely several helpful ideas they can learn from one another (Keith, 2020). The following suggestions could be included in these communications.

BE INVOLVED IN YOUR TEEN'S SCHOOL.

Talk to your school about how they can help you if you are the only one representing your child(ren). If you are unable to attend open house or parent-teacher conferences, ask the school to help you in finding a representative who can attend on your behalf. If your child's teacher cannot accommodate your schedule, suggest an online meeting or another day that works for both of you. Teachers appreciate parents who make an effort to be involved in their child's school life.

KEEP OPEN COMMUNICATION ABOUT HOW YOUR CHILD IS DOING.

Teens, especially, are notorious for saying everything is okay or fine at school when that can be far from the truth. Don't take *okay* for an answer. Ask them specifically about certain subjects, what they are learning, what they like most/least, what seems hardest for them, what class they like most/least, and so on. Then, *listen*. They don't want advice—they just want you to listen. Listening can sometimes be the best gift a parent can give to their child.

DO A MENTAL HEALTH CHECK-IN WITH THEM DAILY.

Just like talking about how school is going, it's important to check in on your child's mental well-being. When you talk to them about this be sure there are no distractions (put the phone away, turn the TV off, stop preparing dinner, avoid checking your watch). If their answer is always "fine," ask them to give you a number from 1 to 5 for how they feel about things going on in their life. Ask open-ended questions that may help them share more information with you. These usually begin with *what* or *how*. Let your teen know that it is okay to talk to you about issues that are sensitive or, if they feel they cannot talk to you, they should seek out

someone who they can. Most teens today are very stressed, so don't be afraid to consult with a counselor at the school if you are concerned about your child's behavior.

VALIDATE YOUR TEEN'S FEELINGS.

Sometimes teens just need parents to accept them for who they are and repeatedly remind them of their strengths and qualities that make them unique. Validate their feelings no matter what those feelings are. If they are angry or depressed, validate that feeling by responding back with something like, "you're _____ that your friend ignored you today." By stating their feeling back to them it lets them know that you are trying to understand their world. Your teen needs to have their emotional bucket filled daily!

BE INVOLVED IN THEIR HOMEWORK.

Be available to answer any questions about school or schoolwork. Be patient and encouraging. Avoid trying to motivate your child through shame-based statements, which can become painful and discouraging to them. Even if you don't have an answer, you can find someone who does. Be resourceful without doing the work for them.

SET UP A SCHEDULE WITH YOUR TEEN.

Children, especially teens, need a schedule. Routines provide a sense of security. Have your teen work with you to set a schoolwork schedule that is reasonable and doable. There will be times when it cannot be followed because of unexpected things that come up, but for the most part it will help by providing more structure and predictability. Teens who have little or no structure or routines are more likely to get into trouble and eventually lose interest in school.

REGULATE TIME ON TECHNOLOGY.

Helping young people with self-regulation skills is so important, especially for today's youth, who are more likely to be addicted to social media and technology. Sit down with your teen and talk about reasonable times for them to be on their phones or devices. Allow them to be part of the decision. Keep technology out of their bedrooms at night so they can get enough uninterrupted sleep. Encourage your teen to find other types of outlets or activities they can do that do not involve technology (board games, sports, walking, hiking, biking, skate-boarding, cooking, reading, journaling, etc.). Having fun with your teen is so important!

COMMUNICATE WITH YOUR TEEN'S SCHOOL AND TEACHERS.

Parent-teacher conferences are very important and are sometimes the only face-to-face time you will get. These meetings will help your child's teacher get to know you better and keep communication more open between you. If you are not able to attend a meeting, be sure to suggest an alternative way to connect. You want to partner with the teachers so that you both share the same expectations for your teenager. Try to communicate some positive things—often teachers only hear complaints from parents. Also, understand the school's discipline policy or behavior expectations. Don't wait until there is an issue to find out the policy.

ENCOURAGE YOUR TEEN'S EFFORTS OVER THEIR PERFORMANCE.

Many young people get stressed out when they don't get all As. There is a lot of pressure to perform in school, and grades are how that is measured. Instead of emphasizing grades, reward your teen's effort in trying to do their best. If they work extremely hard on a test and fail, encourage them by acknowledging how difficult that test must have been. Failing can be good for your teen. It is how they learn and problem-solve from their mistakes. Remember, great inventors succeeded by failing many times. Our culture focuses far too much on showcasing accomplishments such as with grades, trophies, and other tangible rewards. Help your teenager have a positive mindset so they believe they can do it. Your encouragement will go a long way!

Volunteer at school if you are able. It's difficult when you have a full-time job to make time to volunteer at the school. Talk to your employer and see if they are willing to provide some time off and emphasize the importance of being there for your teen. (You could argue that if you are more involved in your teen's life it will mean fewer missed days at work dealing with problems at school.) Maybe you are available to help out at school or become a mentor for another student. These actions can help your teenager see that you care and want to be involved. Besides, your child may behave better when they know you are there.

Attend special events at your teen's school. They may tell you it's not important for you to attend because they sense you are not interested or too busy. *Go!* Your teen really wants you to be part of what they are involved in. If you don't take an interest in their extracurricular activities, they may feel it's not important and quit. Students like when their parents take an interest in their activities. They need experiences where they can be seen as talented at something or hear you say you are proud of their accomplishments.

Encourage your teen's school attendance and involvement. If your teen is having trouble attending school or a particular class, your first step is to talk with them to discover why they are reluctant to attend. Take their attendance seriously so your teen will see that going to school is important. If your child is not involved in anything at school, talk with them about their interests and help find something that fits those interests. If your teen is not connected to some activity, group, or club at school, they are more at risk of dropping out due to disengagement. You may need to talk with the school about helping your teen find an activity that can tap into their personal interests or strengths. If there is nothing that interests them, explore activities offered at a recreation center near where you live or find a church with a strong youth ministry or maybe an organization in your community where they can volunteer. Role model the importance of being involved in activities that interest you.

Advice From Former Dropouts

8

Sometimes the best advice comes from those who have lived the experience. This chapter includes the stories of six former dropouts, in their own words, about their experiences in school, what led them to drop out, and how they got back on track. I encourage you to share these stories with students who have thought about giving up.

Nina

I want to say something to all the teens reading this. I understand how hard high school can become—all the drama, people stepping all over you. You try so hard to do your best, but sometimes you don't have the love and care you wish you could find there. You hang out with the wrong people and make your mom cry. I've been there, done that. I've been through the biggest struggles life has given me. People put you down because you don't have new gear. Fake friends talking about you behind your back. Well, I'm glad I had the chance to say this to whoever is reading it. I do understand. Try not to grow up too quick even though sometimes you're forced to by the struggles. Remember that you must be strong and believe in yourself if nobody else seems to. What you wear isn't who you are. Forget what people think about you, it's your life not theirs. Pick the right friends and choose the right path. You can do it!

Jose

I didn't enjoy school. I found it hard to learn and was always behind. Once I reached high school, I tried school for a couple years before dropping out before my senior year. I decided to help my family by working and started waiting tables. But a couple years later, my girlfriend got pregnant. I then decided it was time to step up and take care of my girlfriend and our new baby on the way.

I found out there weren't any jobs that paid enough to support my new baby. I felt defeated and that I wasted my life working low-paying jobs when continuing my education could have taken me further. I went to adult education in order to earn my GED and work in sales at a car dealership. It's okay to help your family, but don't drop out and ruin your life to do it.

Larissa

I hated school. I felt like the school I was attending wasn't working. I had moved from state to state my whole life. I was a troubled kid; I was never in school. I wanted to be hanging out with "friends." I didn't listen and I disrespected everyone. I got pregnant at 19, had my daughter at 20, then had another at 21. I felt like such a failed mother. I didn't have anything to show them, and I wanted them to be able to say, "Look what my mommy has done." I had goals and dreams to open up my own salon. I finally earned my GED to prove to my kids that I am somebody. Everyone said I was going to fail at life, and I honestly have in some ways, but I worked hard to get my GED and put myself through school to do something I love to do!

It starts with *you*. No matter what your situation is, you can *be a better you*! Believe in yourself and prove that you can do anything you put your mind to!

Travis

I was 17 and wanted to join the Army and go to college. My GED allowed me to do that and much more. My probation counselors motivated me as I was a troubled kid, assigned to a halfway house in Virginia.

My GED allowed me to serve nine years in the Army, finish my bachelor's degree, master's degree, and enroll in school for my doctoral degree. I am currently a school principal at one of the largest youth confinement facilities in Texas, helping kids earn their GEDs. It is what helped me, so I feel in some ways I am returning the hope once given to me.

No matter your age, a GED will help you. It is not simply a replacement for a high school diploma, but a passport to choose your future. Education is a journey, not a destination. Be sure to enjoy the ride.

Anita

When I came to the United States, I only had a seventh-grade education, and English was not my first language. I didn't graduate from high school. I was very embarrassed to tell my friends that I don't have a high school diploma. When I met my husband and his family I lied and said I had a high school diploma. I thought to myself, "I'm not just an illiterate person, but I'm also a liar." I'd only learned how to drop out of high school.

My husband always persuaded me to take the placement exam so I could enroll into college. How could I tell him that I had been lying to him? He trusted me so much that I didn't want to ruin it. I keep telling him that I'm stupid, and that he would just waste the money if he sent me to college. My husband didn't listen to me and kept telling me that I was smart. So, one night I told him the real reason why I didn't want to go to college, it was because I didn't finish high school. I was surprised of his reaction, I expected him to call me a liar, but he just told me to get my GED certificate. I felt a lot better after I told him my deepest secret. I started going to GED classes twice a week. It was really hard for me to learn in the classroom because there were so many people distracting me and I couldn't concentrate.

I decided to research on the internet and found this website called passGED.com. It was the best decision I ever made. It tells you all about techniques in how to pass the GED, and it really helped. Within a few months, I took the GED exam for the first time, and wouldn't you believe it, I passed! I finally was able to start college.

James

My story started when I was in high school. I was a terrible student. I never did any homework, paid attention in class, or studied. I was into having fun, whether it was playing handball, basketball, video games, or spending time with friends.

By 16, I had failed out of high school and had no interest in going back. At 19, I decided to take the GED test. I was too embarrassed to let anyone know I didn't graduate high school. I studied for the test and passed. For the first time in my life, I actually studied.

I decided I was going to try to go to college, but I soon discovered friends, fun, and parties. Three years later I flunked out and was in debt from student loans and school tuition. I was 22, out of school, in debt, and had no degree.

After a few twists and turns in my life, I found myself at 26 years old with nothing to show for it. Through prayer and faith, I went back to college and took prerequisite courses in nursing. After four semesters, I had a 3.5 GPA and applied to the nursing program in Florida. My first three semesters' GPAs were 3.8, 3.9, and 3.7, respectively. I've been a critical care RN for six years. I am currently starting medical school to be an MD. I am proud now to say I went and got my GED. Aim high. You too can do it.

(Stories used with permission from Essential Education)

The Rest of My Story

Immediately after our divorce, Kevin left the state and never contacted the girls again. I moved back to Connecticut and lived for a while with different family members, trying to figure out if I should find full-time work or try to attend a four-year university and earn a degree there. My only option for financial support was applying for welfare again, called Aid to Families with Dependent Children (AFDC) in Connecticut. It was very discouraging when the AFDC department said they could not support me going full time to college. They required that I find a job instead. Trying to find adequate employment and affordable housing to support myself and three children was nearly impossible.

Meanwhile, I received a letter of acceptance from Eastern Connecticut State University. Their only requirement was that I complete a basic English and math class before enrolling as a full-time student. So, I moved again with my girls, now to a subsidized apartment, and started taking these two classes at a community college. I was able to find someone to watch the girls for me while I went to class. Since I couldn't afford to pay her, I cleaned her house in return for her watching my girls.

Once I completed these two classes, I approached AFDC again about attending college full time instead of finding employment. I was determined to convince them that by supporting me for four years I could earn a college degree that would eventually lead to me finding a better job and no longer needing to depend on government assistance. Regardless of my pleas, they continued to decline my request. I decided not to give up and to keep battling my case. I enrolled at the university anyway. I was hoping I would eventually win my argument. Once I started school, I received a further blow from AFDC. Once they learned that I was receiving a Pell

(Continued)

(Continued)

Grant and student loan, they informed me that they considered these funds as "income," which would be deducted from my benefits. However, I remained determined to find some way to keep moving forward, and I appealed my case with them again. In the meantime, I started cleaning houses full time when I wasn't attending classes. However, even with this income, I was barely able to scrape by financially and cover our most basic needs. I felt my situation was becoming hopeless.

I finally received notice that AFDC had reversed its decision about denying my support and would allow me to receive benefits for my girls and me while I attended the university as a full-time student. However, they would still consider my Pell money as income and would continue deducting it from my benefits. Though this was not the outcome I had hoped for, it was enough to allow me to continue moving forward with my plans to eventually earn a college degree.

Attending college, working on the side, taking care of three children, and fighting my battle with AFDC was extremely exhausting. I had to keep telling myself that I could do this; no matter what roadblocks came my way, I would push through and keep moving forward. My girls were a big part of my motivation to continue my efforts. I wanted a better life for them since they had grown up in poverty. I often brought them to classes with me, and most of my professors were very understanding.

I decided to major in sociology. I realized in many of my courses how much information I had missed in high school. I was determined to reach my goal of graduating with a 3.0 GPA. It took four years of going to school full time, including attending classes over the summers, to finally graduate. I finally received a bachelor's degree with a 3.01 GPA. It was like finally having the high school graduation that I never had.

My first job after graduating was working as a state social worker in child protective services. Part of my job was working with the families who had their child(ren) placed in child protective services, which meant I needed to meet weekly with families in person. I used this as an opportunity to talk to them about their goals, especially their own education. Some of my clients believed there was no way they could ever go to college with children still at home and having little financial means. Many had their child(ren) taken away from them and felt it was too late for them to make things right in their life. Fortunately for them, I was a single parent who never graduated from high school and just recently stopped receiving state assistance myself. They were surprised and wanted to know how I had done it.

After 10 years, I eventually met and married my best friend and life coach, Bob Bowman. He encouraged me to continue my education. I attended the University of South Carolina and received an Ed.S. and a LPC licensure. Later I was awarded the Cornelius P. Turner Award, a national honor given yearly to a GED graduate who has made outstanding contributions to society in education, justice, health, public service, or social welfare. I also wrote my memoir, *Breaking Free: A Teenage Runaway's Story of Survival and Triumph* (published through YouthLight). My husband and I share a passion to help troubled youth and started an educational consulting company, Developmental Resources, and a publishing company, YouthLight, Inc. After 30 years, these two companies were sold to AccuTrain and still exist today.

I hope you will use these stories and lessons learned from your own successes in overcoming adversities to encourage your students. Young people are easily motivated by real-life stories of survival and triumph. I passionately believe that our struggles in life are what make us stronger. I am thankful for the opportunities when I can inspire others to know their personal strengths, dream big, and find their purpose in life!

Appendix A

Screening Tool to Identify Students at Higher Risk for Dropping Out

Complete this form for one or more students to determine their risk level for eventually dropping out of school.

0 = Strongly Agree; 1 = Agree; 2 = Somewhat Agree;
3 = Disagree; 4 = Strongly Disagree; 5 = Don't Know

Unmotivated or apathetic toward schoolwork	
Has one or more failing grades	
Has a negative attitude about school	
Self-regulation issues	
Persistently sad or discouraged	
Grief or loss issues	
Has experienced a traumatic event	
Other mental health issues	
History of attendance problems	
Interfering socioeconomic factors exist	
Community violence	
Lacks family support/encouragement	
Presence of mental health issues in family	

(Continued)

(Continued)

Lacks connection with school supports	
Lacks involvement with extracurricular activities	
Socially isolated or alienated	
Lacks short or long-term goals	
Frequent or intense discipline issues	
Anger issues	
Substance abuse issues	
A victim of bullying	
Bullies others	
Anxious or stressed at school	
Issues with social media	
Racial/cultural/gender issues	
Pregnancy	
Lack of resiliency	

Appendix B

Suggested Programs and Initiatives
to Help Students Stay in School

//

Academy of Creative Education

https://www.neisd.net/ace

Accelerated Reader

https://www.renaissance.com/products/accelerated-reader/

Accelerated Schools plus

https://www.acceleratedschools.net

Acceleration Academies

https://info.accelerationacademies.org

ACE Learning Centers

https://acelearningcenters.org

An Achievable Dream

http://achievabledream.nn.k12.va.us/about.html

After School Matters

https://afterschoolmatters.org

Afterschool Alliance

http://www.afterschoolalliance.org

Communities in Schools

https://cisofsc.org

COMPASS Youth Collaborative

https://www.ctopportunityproject.org/partners/compass/

Essential Education

https://www.essentialed.com/educators

Graduation Alliance

https://www.graduationalliance.com/education/education-overview/

Inside-Out Peer Helping

https://insideoutpeerhelping.yolasite.com

I Will Graduate

https://www.iwillgraduateprogram.com/why-2

Jennifer Claire Moore Foundation

https://jennifermoorefoundation.com

Job Corps

https://www.jobcorps.gov

100% Graduation

http://www.mountvernonschools.org/goal

Operation Restart: Getting Dropouts Back on Track

https://www.ednc.org/restart-program-gives-some-low-performing-schools-flexibility-to-help-struggling-students/

Peer Helpers PLUS

https://thriveway.com/pages/peer-helpers

PLUS Program (Peer Leaders Uniting Students)

https://www.stocktonusd.net/domain/174

Positive Action

https://www.positiveaction.net

Putnam County School District: Shaping the Future

https://www.putnamschools.org

Seth Perler

Executive function & ADHD coach, providing resources to help struggling students

https://sethperler.com/freebies/

Renaissance: See Every Student

https://www.renaissance.com/resources/back-to-school/

The 74

www.the74million.org

Synergy Public School

http://www.synergypublicschools.com

Why Try

https://whytry.org/dropout-prevention/

XQ Institute

https://xqsuperschool.org

Appendix C

Famous People Who Faced Challenges But Never Gave Up

///

Albert was born in Germany and struggled in school. He suffered from a learning disability and did not talk until he was four years old. He may have had symptoms of dyslexia. His teachers were discouraged by his slowness in grasping concepts. When he was fifteen his family had to move away, but he stayed in Germany to finish his education at a preparatory school there. He eventually became one of the most famous and influential scientists of all times. *Albert Einstein*

Temple struggled as a child. At two years old she couldn't speak and was diagnosed with severe autism. She endured many hours of speech therapy and rigorous teaching to learn how to speak. As a teen she endured constant teasing. After the help of a high school science teacher, she went on to pursue a career as a scientist and received a PhD in animal science. She has received numerous awards, written several books, and had a movie made about her life. Her design of livestock handling facilities that reduce stress for animals has been used worldwide. She is known as one of "the 100 most influential people in the world." *Temple Grandin*

Gabby grew up in a single-parent home. She was six years old when she started gymnastics. She was home-schooled starting in third grade. For years, she endured racially offensive bullying at her gym, to the point where she considered leaving gymnastics for good. She moved out of state at the age of fourteen to go to another gym. Her mom and sister were not financially able to go with her, so she had to live with a host family while training there. She overcame the bullying and harassment and went on to become an Olympic gold medal gymnast and a national role model for girls everywhere. *Gabby Douglas*

Jose was born in Mexico and traveled back and forth to the USA to work with his family and other migrant workers in California harvesting crops. He attended many different schools as he traveled with his family and worked. He learned to speak English when he was twelve. He also managed to go to college and graduate with both a bachelor's and master's degree. He applied to NASA eleven times but was rejected. He never gave up his dream to be an astronaut, and finally in 2004, he was accepted and was the first former migrant farmworker to have traveled to space. *José Hernández*

Christine's early home life was troubled. Her father was physically and emotionally abusive, and music was her only escape. By the time she was in elementary school, her talented voice caused her schoolmates and even some parents to envy her. She was eventually homeschooled to avoid the bullying she experienced at school. She is not only a Grammy Award–winning singer, but also a songwriter, record producer, actress, and dancer. *Christina Aguilera*

Steven moved repeatedly with his family and fell two years behind his classmates, making average grades in school. He was a victim of anti-Semitic bullying so much that he dreaded going to school. In high school his low grades kept him from getting into a major university. He did eventually graduate from a state college. He is known worldwide for many famous movies and has been nominated for numerous awards as an American film director, producer, and screenwriter. *Steven Spielberg*

Famous People Who Earned a GED

Christina Applegate

David Bowie

Nicolas Cage

Cher

Sean Connery

50 Cent

Carrie Fisher

Michael J. Fox

Gene Hackman

George Harrison

Paris Hilton

Peter Jennings

Angelina Jolie

Lindsay Lohan

Loretta Lynn

Bam Margera

Kelly McGillis

Pink

Chris Rock

Michelle Rodriquez

Jessica Simpson

Christian Slater

Britney Spears

Hilary Swank

John Travolta

Mark Wahlberg

(From Dannielle Doyle, President Student Division 2023; Ranker, 2021)

Appendix D

Quotes to Encourage Students at Risk for Dropping Out

///

Here are some famous quotes that we need to share with those students who either fail to try or try and fail to encourage them to not give up so quickly. Tell them to post their favorite quotes on their phones/devices or print them and stick them on their mirrors at home.

"Never get discouraged if you fail. Learn from it. Keep trying."
–Thomas Edison

"The only way to achieve the impossible is to believe it is possible."

–Alice in Wonderland

"Don't let anyone rob you of your imagination, your creativity, or your curiosity. It's your place in the world; it's your life. Go on and do all you can with it and make it the life you want to live."
–Mae Jemison, engineer, physician, and former NASA astronaut

"Most of the important things in the world have been accomplished by people who have kept on trying when there seemed to be no hope at all."

–Dale Carnegie

"We need to accept that we won't always make the right decisions, that we'll screw up royally sometimes—understanding that failure is not the opposite of success, it's part of success."

–Arianna Huffington

"Strength does not come from winning. Your struggles develop your strengths. When you go through hardships and decide not to surrender, that is true strength."

—Arnold Schwarzenegger

"Obstacles don't have to stop you. If you run into a wall, don't turn around and give up. Figure out how to climb it, go through it, or work around it."

—Michael Jordan

"We may encounter many defeats, but we must not be defeated."

—Maya Angelou

"There will be obstacles. There will be doubters. There will be mistakes. But with hard work, there are no limits."

—Michael Phelps

"Never give up, for that is just the place and time that the tide will turn."

—Harriet Beecher Stowe

"If you can't fly, then run. If you can't run, then walk. If you can't walk, then crawl. But whatever you do, you have to keep moving forward."

—Martin Luther King Jr.

"Do not fear failure but rather fear not trying."

—Roy T. Bennett

"If you don't go after what you want, you'll never have it. If you don't ask, the answer is always no. If you don't step forward, you're always in the same place."

—Nora Roberts

"Education is the key to unlock the golden door of freedom."

—George Washington Carver

"If you fall behind, run faster. Never give up, never surrender, and rise up against the odds."

—Jesse Jackson

"The purpose of education is to turn mirrors into windows."
–Sydney J. Harris

"Don't close the book when bad things happen in your life!
Just turn the page and start a new chapter!"
–LaToya Jackson

"Getting knocked down in life is a given. Getting up and
moving forward is a choice!"
–Zig Ziglar

"We do not need magic to change the world, we carry all
the power we need inside ourselves already: we have the
power to imagine better."
–J. K. Rowling, author

"If people tell you that you can't, then show them that you can
and if they say you will never amount to anything then
show them your worth."
–Susan Bowman

"You should never give up your inner self."
–Clint Eastwood

"The biggest risk is not taking any risk. . . . In a world
that's changing really quickly, the only strategy that is
guaranteed to fail is not taking risks."
–Mark Zuckerberg

"The question isn't who's going to let me; it's who is going to
stop me."
–Ayn Rand

"I don't know what the future holds, but I do know that I'm
going to be positive and not wake up feeling desperate."
–Billie Jean King

"Have I not commanded you? Be strong and courageous.
Do not be afraid; do not be discouraged, for the Lord your
God will be with you wherever you go."
–Joshua 1:9 The Bible

"Education is the most powerful weapon which you can use to change the world."

–Nelson Mandela

"The content of a book holds the power of education, and it is with this power that we can shape our future and change lives."

–Malala Yousafzai

Appendix E

"The Old Leather Jacket"

A Teacher's Powerful Impact

Mrs. McGloughlin was a fifth-grade teacher at Sandhill Middle School. She had been teaching at the same school for 12 years and was known for being highly organized, structured, and confident in her classroom management skills.

It was the beginning of the school year, and all teachers were required to report to school a week before the students arrived. She was handed her roster and noticed a name that caused her some concern. It was a student who was mentioned quite frequently in the teacher's breakroom for being a "troublemaker with a capital T": Russell Hubbert. It didn't help when another teacher said to her, "Buckle up because you are headed for a disaster!" This made her even more anxious about the upcoming school year.

Russell was a respectable student with decent grades in the early years. She came across a few school photos from his early years in kindergarten to second grade where he had the biggest smile, in a pressed dress shirt with a groomed haircut. When she looked at his third- and fourth- grade file, she noticed a big difference in his grades, mostly Ds. Looking at his fourth-grade pictures she noticed that instead of a big smile Russell had an expression that said he did not want his picture taken. By fifth grade, his eyes were looking away, his lips were pressed together, his hair was long and ungroomed, and he wore an old black leather jacket. Because of his many absences and failing grades, he was repeating fifth grade. She couldn't help wondering what happened to cause Russell to decline so drastically. Fourth grade was characterized by chronic absenteeism, a defiant attitude toward adults, refusal to do any class work, sarcasm, and bullying behavior toward other students. She was not looking forward to the challenging year that lay ahead.

Mrs. McGloughlin was determined to start this year with firm and clear expectations. She knew if she was too soft at the beginning of the year she would regret it later.

The first day for students had arrived. They walked into the room and found a place to sit. Those who knew others in their class from the previous year sat together. Some were excited and sat closer to the front of the room. The last student to enter the classroom was Russell Hubbert. He wore an oversized black leather jacket and shuffled his way to the back of the room, plopped down in a chair, and leaned back with his feet teetering on the edge of the desk. Mrs. McGloughlin could see some of the students whispering to one another while some just rolled their eyes or shook their head as if to say, *not him again!* The teacher spoke loudly, "Okay, everyone—let's settle down."

Mrs. McGloughlin greeted her class and told the students to review the rules she placed on the front of her desk. She explained in detail what each rule meant so there would be no confusion. Suddenly, Russell interrupted her insisting that there had been a mistake. He said he is supposed to be in sixth grade and doesn't know why they put him in her fifth-grade class. She calmly asked him to wait until the class was dismissed to talk more about it. After the bell sounded and the students left the room, she walked over to Russell and asked him why he thinks he is in the wrong grade. He told her that he was older than the other students and was never told that he would be repeating the fifth grade. She explained that because he had failing grades and was absent for so many days, he could not be promoted to the next grade. He was noticeably angry and stormed out of her classroom.

On the second day of school, Russell had an altercation with another student. He was sent to the principal's office and from there he was sent to in-school suspension for the remainder of that day and the next day as well. This didn't seem to bother him since he preferred being in a smaller class.

On day 3, Mrs. McGloughlin was relieved that Russell was not there to disrupt the class so she could actually teach. After class she started to think that maybe she got off on the wrong foot with Russell. So, she decided to call his home to talk with his parents. A woman answered and said she was Russell's mother. She explained that Russell's dad left several years ago, and he did not have any contact with him since. After Mrs. McGloughlin had a conversation with Russell's mother, she started to understand his situation more and realized what was causing some of his behavior at school. She decided that she was going to try a different approach with class to encourage more student interaction.

The day that Russell returned to class she passed out sticky notes to everyone and asked them to write three things they were good at or had an interest in. She explained how these things needed to be positive and if they couldn't think of three to write two. She could see that Russell wasn't writing anything on his sticky note. She made her way to where he was sitting and said, "Russell I know you must have at least one interest or hobby you are good at—how about writing at least one down?" He reluctantly sat up and wrote something on the sticky note. After the students all wrote on their notes, they were asked to stick it on their shoulder or head and stand up and walk around the room to find another person who shared at least one of the same interests. When they found someone who matched the same thing as them, they were to stand next to them. Mrs. McGloughlin looked around the room and noticed that Russell was standing next to someone! She asked for students to share the name of the person they stood with and what their mutual interest was. Russell introduced his partner and stated that their mutual interest was art. Mrs. McGloughlin then asked for students to share with that person why they had their particular interest and what they liked most about it. After the activity the students went back to their desk. When Mrs. McGloughlin asked the class to share what they learned from doing this activity, she heard statements such as, *learning something we didn't know about others, what we have in common,* and *how to get to know others better.*

The next day when the students entered her classroom, she handed them a blank index card and asked each student to write one thing that worries or stresses them. She explained that it could be about school or something personal. The students quietly wrote on their cards. She asked the students to flip their cards over once they finished writing and went around and collected all the notes and mixed them up. She read them aloud, asking students to raise their hand if they had ever experienced that particular worry or concern. She skipped over those that had the same thing written on it, but by time she read through the notes, most students had raised their hands. She took notice that Russell raised his hand the most. When she finished, she asked the students what they learned. The responses included *many of us worry about the same things, we are not alone in what we worry about, we don't always talk about things that worry us,* and *it's okay to share our worries.*

By the end of the second week, the students were interacting more with each other and even Russell was starting to feel a part of the class. Mrs. McGloughlin told the class that from now on if any of them came to class worried or stressed about something, she was going to have cards available for them to write their concern on along with their name and a box for them to drop their note into. She also met more frequently with Russell, making sure to tell him something positive she noticed that he did that day or week. Once she knew he liked art, she asked him if he could lead an art project for their classroom hallway. He really took pride in being involved in something he was good at.

As the year went on, she noticed Russell's grades had improved. His Ds were now Cs and he was receiving individual tutoring after school, which really helped him. She also noticed another strength that Russell had. He was very good in helping others who were experiencing problems. She asked him if he would be interested in joining their school's Peer Helper program. Russell went through the training and started meeting with students regularly. He learned by helping others how to cope better and think before acting out. In time, his reputation changed from being a troublemaker with a capital T to a peer helper with a capital P!

The next year Russell was promoted to sixth grade. He continued his involvement with the Peer Helper program and was asked to mentor a fourth-grade student who was experiencing some behavior problems. When Russell met with this student and learned he also had a dad who was not involved in his life, he understood where this student was coming from. It made Russell feel good that he could help turn around a troubled student. He had confidence in himself and looked forward to graduating from high school one day. On the last day of middle school, he handed a note to Mrs. McGloughlin while thanking her for helping him get through a tough time and believing in him. He told her to not read the note he gave her until the day he graduated from high school. Although she said it would be very difficult to wait that long, she would do as he asked. Russell started high school with more friends than he ever had. He had a little difficulty transitioning to ninth grade but knew to ask for a tutor to help him. He made more friends and even found some after-school activities to be involved in.

By time he was a senior, he helped to start a peer mentoring program and mentored several struggling ninth graders. He stopped by to visit Mrs. McGloughlin a couple of times to tell her how he was doing. He went by one last time to see her and hand her an invitation to his high school graduation. Mrs. McGloughlin was so happy to hear that he was graduating and told Russell that she would be honored to be there to see him receive his high school diploma. She asked him if she could bring the letter with her that he wrote her four years earlier. Russell was so happy that she still had it and told her that she could open it after the graduation.

On graduation day, Russell's mom and grandmother were there to see him earn his high school diploma. Right beside his mom and grandmother was his former teacher, Mrs. McGloughlin. Russell also received a scholarship to a college close by and decided he wanted to pursue a career in counseling to help other kids who struggled in school like he did. He always gave credit to his fifth-grade teacher, Mrs. McGloughlin, for caring and believing him when no one else would.

Mrs. McGloughlin did finally open that envelope Russell gave her when he left middle school. This is what the letter said:

> Thank you, Mrs. McGloughlin, for not giving up on me when I was an angry and defiant child. I was so angry the day my dad left us. What you didn't know is that the leather jacket I wore every day belonged to my dad. It was all I had to remember him by. That day I walked into class after in-school suspension was the day I had seriously considered not going to school anymore. I was so stressed at home seeing my mom so sad and not understanding why my dad left us. I took my anger out on others and I felt that no one really cared if I was at school. I only thought about being with my dad again and was mad that I couldn't make that happen. The day you asked us to write something we were good at or interested in made me nervous because I thought others in class didn't like me. I never felt like anyone cared about me and only saw me as a troublemaker. When you came to my desk and encouraged me to think of something I was good at I felt for the first time someone cared. Once I found that a couple other students also liked art, I felt I had something in common with others. That day I went home and instead of being discouraged and feeling sad, I took out a piece of paper and decided to draw you a picture. It had been a while since I drew anything, but it felt good to express my feelings in my drawings.

She then opened up a folded piece of paper that was included in the envelope. It was a sketch Russell did that year of a rose that included such beautiful detail it brought tears to her eyes. There was a note on the bottom that said,

This rose is a reminder of the hope you gave me to keep going and to not give up. The day you had the class write down concerns we had, I wrote that I was worried I would never graduate from high school. I decided to wait to give you this letter and drawing as a promise to myself that I would one day graduate. Thanks for waiting to open this letter just like you waited for me to finally show you my true potential. You encouraged me to use my strengths to help others and when I did it made me feel good about myself. I wish all teachers could be just like you! I will always remember you.

Love,
Russell

References

Abrams, Z. (2023, August 25). Discipline is still biased. How to reduce racial disparities in suspension rates. *Monitor on Psychology*, *54*(7). www.apa.org/monitor/2023/10/racial-disparities-suspension-rates

Acceleration Academies. (2022, October). *What happens if I drop out of high school?* https://accelerationacademies.org

Allison, M., & Attisha, E. (2019). The link between school attendance and good health. *American Academy of Pediatrics*, *143*(2).

Alvarez, B. (2021). *School suspensions do more harm than good. NEA Today.* https://nea.org/nea-today/all-news-articles/school-suspensions-do-more-harm-good

American Civil Liberties Union (ACLU). (2023). *School-to-prison pipeline.* https://www.aclu.org/issues/juvenile-justice/juvenile-justice-school-prison-pipeline

American Psychological Association (APA). (2022). *Exploring the mental health effects of poverty, hunger, and homelessness on children and teens.* https://apa.org/topics/socioeconomic-status/poverty-hunger-homelessness-children

American School Counselor Association. (2019). *ASCA School Counselor Professional Standards & Competencies.* Alexandria, VA.

American School Counselor Association. (2022). *ASCA ethical standards for school counselors.* https://schoolcounselor.org/getmedia/44f30280-ffe8-4b41-9ad8-f1590 9c3d164/EthicalStandards.pdf

American School Counselor Association. (2024). *The ASCA national model: What the research says.* https://schoolcounselor.org/getmedia/d8716b30-9a5e-4de3-8af0-6 1fb76de57c2/ANM-Effectiveness-Research.pdf

Anderson, M., Vogels, E., Perrin, A., & Rainie, L. (2022). *Connection, creativity and drama: Teen life on social media in 2022.* Pew Research Center. https://www.pewresearch.org/internet/2022/11/16/connection-creativity-and-drama-teen-life-on-social-media-in-2022/

Annie E. Casey Foundation. (2022). *Child well-being in single-parent families.* Annie E. Casey Foundation Blog. https://aecf.org/blog/child-well-being-in-single-parent-families

Annie E. Casey Foundation. (2023). *2020 high school graduation rate held steady despite pandemic disruptions.* Annie E. Casey Foundation Blog. https://aecf.org/blog/2020-high-school-graduation-rate-held-steady-despite-pandemic-disruptions#:~:text=The%209 latest%20data%20from%20the,indicator%20 of%20youth%20well%2Dbeing

Barrington, K. (2023). What is the impact of high school graduation rates? *Public School Review.* https://www.publicschoolreview.com/blog/what-is-the-impact-of-high-school-graduation-rates

Bowman, R. P. (2024, March 9). Meaningful magic, props and metaphors. [featured presentation], *Innovative Schools Summit 2024*, Orlando FL.

Bowman, R. P., & Bowman, S. (2019). *Meaningful mentoring: A handbook of effective* strategies, projects and activities. Youth-Light, Inc. www.youthlight.com

Bowman, S. (2021). *Helping adolescents know what to do when a peer is in crisis.* YouthLight, Inc. www.youthlight.com

Bridgeland, J., Dilulio, J., & Morison, K. B. (2006). The silent epidemic: Perspectives of high school dropouts. https://docs.gatesfoundation.org/documents/thesilentepidemic3-06final.pdf

Brown, C., Boser, U., & Sargrad, S. (2016). *Implementing the Every Student Succeeds Act: Toward a coherent, aligned assessment system.* Center for American Progress. https://americanprogress.org/article/implementing-the-every-student-succeeds-act/

Bushnell, L. (2021). *Educational disparities among racial and ethnic minority youth in the United States.* Ballard Brief. https://scholarsarchive.byu.edu/ballardbrief/vol2021/iss2/9/

Centers for Disease Control and Prevention (CDC). (2021). *Poor mental health impacts adolescent well-being.* https://cdc.gov/healthyyouth

Centers for Disease Control and Prevention (CDC). (2023a). *Youth risk behavior surveillance system report.* www.cdc.gov/healthyyouth/data/yrbs/pdf/YRBS_Data-Summary-Trends_Report2023_508.pdf

Centers for Disease Control and Prevention (CDC). (2023b). *School connectedness.* www.cdc.gov/healthyschools/school_connectedness.htm

Chatterjee, R. (2022). Kids are back in school and struggling with mental health issues. *NPR. Health News.* www.npr.org/sections/health-shots/2022/01/07/1070969456/kids-are-back-in-school-and-struggling-with-mental-health-issues

Chen, G. (2022). What is race to the top and how will it benefit public schools? *Public School Review.* https://publicschoolreview.com/blog/what-is-race-to-the-top-and-how-will-it-benefit-public-schools

Chilton, J. I. (2023). *Reversing the "school-to-prison pipeline"? Part 1: Defining the school-to-prison pipeline.* Close Up. Washington DC. https://closeup.org/reversing-the-school-to-prison-pipeline-part-1-defining-the-school-to-prison-pipeline/

Clark, G. (2022). *Restorative justice not school suspensions: Disciplinary reforms help students and teachers connect.* The Education Trust. https://edtrust.org/the-equity-line/restorative-justice-not-school-suspensions-disciplinary-reforms-help-students-and-teachers-connect/

Creamer, J., Shrider, E., Burns, K., & Chen, F. (2022). *Poverty in the United States: 2021.* United States Census Bureau. https://census.gov/library/publications/2022/demo/p60-277.html

Daniel, S. S., Walsh, A. K., Goldston, D. B., Arnold, E. M., Reboussin, B. A., & Wood, F. B. (2006). Suicidality, school dropout, and reading problems among adolescents. *Journal of Learning Disabilities, 39*(6): 507–14. https://doi.org/10.1177/00222194060390060301. PMID: 17165618.

Duckworth, A. (2016). *Grit: The power of passion and perseverance.* Simon & Schuster.

Drug Enforcement Administration (DEA). (2023). *School failure.* Get Smart about Drugs. www.getsmartaboutdrugs.gov/content/school-failure

Edwards, D. (1995). The school counselor's role in helping teachers and students belong. *Elementary School Guidance & Counseling, 29*(3).

Edwards, E., & Jackson, H. (2023, May). Social media is driving teen mental health crisis, surgeon general warns. *NBC News.* https://nbcnews.com/health/health-news/social-media-mental-health-anxiety-depression-teens-surgeon-general-rcna85575

Excel High School. (2023, March 15). *7 successful people who finished high school later in life.* www.excelhighschool.com/blog/7-successful-people-who-finished-high-school-later-in-life

Fikac, N., & Bowman, R. P. (2024). *1-minute encouragers for educators.* YouthLight, Inc. www.youthlight.com

Gewertz, C. (2022). H.S. dropouts say lack of motivation top reasons to quit. *Education Week.* https://www.edweek.org/teaching-learning/h-s-dropouts-say-lack-of-motivation-top-reason-to-quit/2006/03

Giano, Z., Williams, A., & Becnel, J. (2022). Grade retention and school dropout: Comparing specific grade levels across childhood and early adolescence. *Journal of Early Adolescence, 42*(1). https://journals.sagepub.com/doi/10.1177/02724316211010332

Glazer, N. T. (1978). Reading deficiency and behavior problems: A study. *Reading Horizons: A Journal of Literacy and Language Arts, 18*(4). https://scholarworks.wmich.edu/reading_horizons/vol18/iss4/8

Goldhaber, D., Kane, T., McEachin, A., Patterson, T., & Staiger, D. (2022). *The consequences of remote and hybrid instruction during the pandemic.* Cambridge, MA: Center for Education Policy Research, Harvard University. https://cepr.harvard.edu/files/cepr/files/5-4.pdf?m=1651690491

Goodwin, B. (2021). Research matters/does restorative justice work? *ASCD, 79*(2). https://ascd.org/el/articles/research-matters-does-restorative-justice-work

Gu, W., Zhao, Q., Yuan, C., Yi, Z., Zhao, M., & Wang, Z. (2022). Impact of adverse childhood experiences on the symptom severity of different mental disorders: a cross-diagnostic study. *General Psychiatry, 35*(2). www.ncbi.nlm.nih.gov/pmc/articles/PMC9036421

Haidt, J. (2024). *The anxious generation: How the great rewiring of childhood is causing an epidemic of mental illness.* New York: Penguin Press.

Hale, L., & Canter, A. (2023, March). *School dropout prevention-strategies for educators.* NASP Center. https://naspcenter.org/factsheets/school-dropout-prevention/#

Henderson, A., & Mapp, K. (2022). *A new wave of evidence: The impact of school, family, and community connections on student achievement.* Annual Synthesis 2002. National Center for Family and Community Connections with Schools. Austin, TX. https://sedl.org/connections/resources/evidence.pdf

Hendrick, C. E., & Maslowsky, J. (2019). Teen mothers' educational attainment and their children's risk for teenage childbearing. *Developmental Psychology, 55*(6), 1259–73. https://psycnet.apa.org/doiLanding?doi=10.1037%2Fdev0000705

Hilliard, J. (2024). *Social media addiction.* Addiction Center. www.addictioncenter.com/drugs/social-media-addiction

Hirschfeld, J. (2008). *What if we closed the title I comparability loophole?* Center for American Progress. https://www.americanprogress.org/article/what-if-we-closed-the-title-i-comparability-loophole/

Kamenetz, A., & Turner, C. (2016). *The high school graduation rate reaches a record high-again.* NPR. https://npr.org/sections/ed/2016/10/17/498246451/the-high-school-graduation-reaches-a-record-high-again

Keith, K. L. (2020). How parents can become more involved in schools. *Verywellfamily.* https://www.verywellfamily.com/parent-involvement-in-schools-619348

Klein, A. (2015). No Child Left Behind: An overview. *Education Week.* https://www.edweek.org/policy-politics/no-child-left-behind-an-overview/2015/04

Klevan, S. (2021). *Building a positive school climate through restorative practices.* Learning Policy Institute. https://doi.org/10.54300/178.861

Kuhfeld, M., Soland, J., & Lewis, K. (2022). *Test score patterns across three COVID-19 impacted school years.* (EdWorkingPaper: 22-521). Retrieved from Annenberg Institute at Brown University, https://doi.org/10.26300/ga82-6v47

Lansford, J. E., Lansford, J., Dodge, K., Pettit, G., & Bates, J. (2016). A public health perspective on school dropout and adult outcomes: A prospective study of risk and protective factors from age 5 to 27 years. *Journal of Adolescent Health, 58*(6): 652–8. https://pubmed.ncbi.nlm.nih.gov/27009741/

Leeb, R. T., Bitsko, R., Radhakrishnan, L., Martinez, P., Njai, R., & Holland, K. (2020). Mental health–related emergency department visits among children aged <18 years during the COVID-19 pandemic—United States. *MMWR: Morbidity and Mortality Weekly Report, 69*: 1675–80. https://cdc.gov/mmwr/volumes/69/wr/mm6945a3.htm?s_cid=mm6945a3_w#suggestedcitation

Lee-St. John, T. J., Walsh, M. E., Raczek, A. E., Vuilleumier, C. E., Foley, C., Heberle, A., Sibley, E., & Dearing, E. (2018, October–December). The long-term impact of systemic student support in elementary school: Reducing high school dropout. *AERA Open*, *4*(4). https://journals.sagepub.com/doi/epub/10.1177/2332858418799085

Leung-Gagné, M., McCombs, J., Scott, C., & Losen, D. J. (2022). Pushed out: Trends and disparities in out-of-school suspension. https://learningpolicyinstitute.org/sites/default/files/2022-09/CRDC_School_Suspension_REPORT.pdf

Lieberman, M. (2022). The COVID school-relief funds you might not know about, explained. *Education Week*. https://edweek.org/policy-politics/the-covid-school-relief-funds-you-might-not-know-about-explained/2022/08

Long, C. (2017, December 19). Some of the surprising reasons why students drop out of school. *NEA Today*. https://nea.org/nea-today/all-news-articles/some-surprising-reasons-why-students-drop-out-school

Mayo Clinic. (2022). *Teen depression*. https://mayoclinic.org/diseases-conditions/teen-depression/symptoms-causes/syc-20350985

McCullough, V. (2021). *When mental health struggles cause issues at school*. Idaho Connects Online School. https://www.i-conschool.org/blog/when-mental-health-struggles-cause-struggles-at-school

Miller, R. (2021, November 22). *Meet the 88-year-old who just became the oldest to earn GED from Easton program*. Lehighvalleylive.com. https://www.lehighvalleylive.com/news/2021/11/meet-the-88-year-old-who-just-became-the-oldest-to-earn-ged-from-easton-program.html

Moscoviz, L., & Evans, D. (2022). *Learning loss and student dropouts during the COVID-19 pandemic: A review of the evidence two years after schools shut down*. Center for Global Development. https://cgdev.org/sites/default/files/learning-loss-and-student-dropouts-during-covid-19-pandemic-review-evidence-two-years.pdf

Mphaphuli, L. K. (2023). *The impact of dysfunctional families on the mental health of children*. IntechOpen. https://doi.org/10.5772/intechopen.110565.

National Center for Education Statistics (NCES). (2022). *Roughly half of public schools report that they can effectively provide mental health services to all students in need*. NCES. https://nces.ed.gov/whatsnew/press_releases/05_31_2022_2.asp

National Center for Education Statistics (NCES). (2024). *Status dropout rates. Condition of education*. U.S. Department of Education, Institute of Education Sciences. https://nces.ed.gov/programs/coe/indicator/coj

National Conference of State Legislatures (NCSL). (2018). *Teen pregnancy prevention*. https://ncsl.org/health/teen-pregnancy-prevention

Osbourne, N. (2023). *Does social media impact teen substance abuse?* American Addiction Centers. https://americanaddictioncenters.org/blog/does-social-media-impact-teen-substance-use

Paul, C. A. (2017). *Elementary and secondary education act of 1965. Social Welfare History Project*. Virginia Commonwealth University. https://socialwelfare.library.vcu.edu/programs/education/elementary-and-secondary-education-act-of-1965/

Perera, R., & Diliberti, M. K. (2023). *Survey: Understanding how U.S. public schools approach school discipline. Brown Center on Education Policy*. Brookings. https://brookings.edu/articles/survey-understanding-how-us-public-schools-approach-school-discipline/

Radevska, I. (2021). How family mental health affects child development. *Parenting and Family Mental Health*. https://rtor.org/2021/11/15/how-family-mental-health-affects-child-development/

Rex, J., Rex, S., Bowman, R. P., & Bowman, S. (2022). *Helping anxious and discouraged youth*. YouthLight, Inc.

Rothwell, J. (2023). *How parenting and self-control mediate the link between social media use and youth mental health*.

Institute for Family Studies and Gallup. https://ifstudies.org/ifs-admin/resources/briefs/ifs-gallup-parentingsocialmediascreentime-october2023-1.pdf

Schreiber, D. (1964). *Guidance and the school dropout*. National Education Association of the United States. LOC. 64-16324. Washington, DC. https://files.eric.ed.gov/fulltext/ED079643.pdf

Serani, D. (2020). Depression and school dropout rates: Knowing risk factors and protective factors. *Psychology Today*. https://psychologytoday.com/us/blog/two-takes-on-depression/202008/depression-and-school-drop-out-rates

Sparks, S. (2011). Study: Third grade reading predicts later high school graduation. *Education Week*. www.edweek.org/teaching-learning/study-third-grade-reading-predicts-later-high-school-graduation/2011/04

Sparks, S. (2021). Is the bottom falling out for readers who struggle the most? *Education Week*. www.edweek.org/teaching-learning/is-the-bottom-falling-out-for-readers-who-struggle-the-most/2021/06

Sparks, S. (2022). Plunging graduation rates signal long recovery. *Education Week*. https://edweek.org/teaching-learning/plunging-graduation-rates-signal-long-recovery/2022/08

Torres, S. (2020). After coronavirus, expect high school dropout wave. 9/11 was the trigger for my sisters. *USA Today*. https://usatoday.com/story/opinion/2020/04/30/coronavirus-school-closings-lifelong-consequences-teens-column/3047910001/

Truth in American Education. (2023, June 10). What happens if you drop out of high school? *American Education*. https://truthinamericaneducation.com/what-happens-if-you-drop-out-of-high-school/

U.S. Department of the Treasury. (2023, June 9). *Post 5: Racial differences in educational experiences and attainment*. Office of Economic Policy. https://home.treasury.gov/news/featured-stories/post-5-racial-differences-in-educational-experiences-and-attainment

U.S. Surgeon General's Advisory. (2023). *Social media and youth mental health*. https://www.hhs.gov/surgeongeneral/priorities/youth-mental-health/social-media/index.html

Varenhorst, B. (1992). Why peer helping? *Peer Facilitator Quarterly*, *10*(2). https://vesper.org/wp-content/uploads/DOC121814.pdf

Véronneau, M.-H., & Trempe, S.-C. (2024). The quality of the relationship with a best friend and the risk of dropping out of high school: Mediating effects of academic motivation. *Canadian Journal of Behavioural Science*. APA Psycnet. https://psycnet.apa.org/record/2023-28106-001

What is goals 2000: The Educate America Act? (1994). *Council For Exceptional Children*, *27*(1), 78–80. https://doi.org/10.1177/004005999402700117

Wildsmith, E., Welti, K., Finocharo, J., & Ryberg, R. (2022, December 23). The 30-year decline in teen birth rates has accelerated since 2010. *Child Trends*. https://www.childtrends.org/blog/the-30-year-decline-in-teen-birth-rates-has-accelerated-since-2010

Wilkins N., Krause, K., Verlenden, J., Szucs, L., Ussery, E., Allen, C., Stinson, J., Michael, S., & Ethier, K. (2023). School connectedness and risk behaviors and experiences among high school students—youth risk behavior survey, United States, 2021. *MMWR* Suppl, 2023; *72* (Suppl-1):13–21. http://dx.doi.org/10.15585/mmwr.su7201a2

Index

Academic challenges, 11
Acceleration Academies, 8, 23
Adverse childhood experiences (ACEs), 3, 15
Aid to Families with Dependent Children
    (AFDC), 85–86
American Psychological Association
    (APA), 16, 17
American School Counselor Association's
    (ASCA), 42–43, 53, 56
Annie E. Casey Foundation, 17

Barrington, K., 8
Bowman, S., 101
Bridgeland, J., 28
Bullycide, 39
Bullying/school violence, 14

Centers for Disease Control and Prevention
    (CDC), 15
Chronic absenteeism, 3, 14, 31
Chronic discipline problem, 12
Connecticut, 85
Connecticut National Guard, 27
Connections through school, 8
Connect With a Suicide & Crisis Counselor, 39
Counseling groups, 53–56
COVID-19 pandemic, 1, 6 (figure)
Cultural disparity, 16

Daily mental health check-in, 78
Digital detox, 14
Dilulio, J., 28
Disconnection, 11–12
Disengagement, 11–12
Drop-in center, 3
Dropout prevention, strategies to, 73–76
Dropping out
    case studies, 9

impact of, 7–9
national education initiatives, 6 (figure)
students screening tool, 89–90
Drug Enforcement Administration (DEA), 16

Educators, 64
Elementary and Secondary Education Act
    (ESSA), 6 (figure)

Family mental/physical health issues, 15
Famous people challenges, 95–97
Fast-paced generation, 18
Former dropouts advice, 81–84
Fostering resiliency, 18–19
Frequent (discipline) flyers, 12

Goals 2000: Educate America Act, 6 (figure)
Governor's Emergency Education Relief Fund, 6
    (figure)
Grit, lack of, 18–19

Home visits, 59–60
Homework involvement, 78

Impulsive behavior, 34
In-school suspensions (ISSs), 2, 50
Inspiration, family and friends, 9

Language, 16
Learning disability, 2
Learning from students, 21–39
    recommended strategies, 29, 38–39
    school dropouts personal stories, 29–30
Learning Policy Institute, 50
LGBQ+ students, 41–42

Missouri Model, 53
Multi-tiered systems of support (MTSS), 51

National Alliance on Mental Illness (NAMI), 47
National Conference of State Legislatures
    (NCSL), 17
National Dropout Prevention Center, 6 (figure)
No Child Left Behind Act (NCLB), 6 (figure)

Old leather jacket, 103–108
Open communication, 78
Opportunities
    school, 8
    work, 8

Parent/guardian involvement
    daily mental health check-in, 78
    homework involvement, 78
    open communication, 78
    regulate time on technology, 79
    teen schedule, 78
    teen's efforts, 79–80
    teen's feelings validating, 78
    teen's school and teachers
        communications, 79
    teen's school involvement, 78
Peer influence, 15–16
Peer support, 67–71
Personal freedom desire, 19–20
Personal strengths
    purpose, 61–63
    words, 63, 65
Personal support system, 52–53
Positive behavioral intervention and supports
    (PBIS), 51
Poverty, 17
Pregnancy, 17–18
Public School Review (PSR), 7

Quotes, students encouragement, 99–102

Race to the Top (RTT) funding, 6 (figure)
Racism, 16
Red flags, 38
Resiliency, 18–19
Restorative circles, 51
Restorative discipline practices, 50–52
Risk of dropping out
    counseling groups, 53–56
    home visits, 59–60
    personal strengths and purpose, 61–63
    personal support system, 52–53
    restorative discipline practices, 50–52

small support, 53–56
student peer helping and mentoring, 56–59
students avoid seeking help from others,
    43–48
students find/create connection, 48–50
students mental health needs, 41–43

School dropping out, 1
School resource officers (SROs), 50
School resources/supports, lack of, 12
School-to-prison pipeline, 12
Self-confidence, 9, 61
Self-encouraging mindset, 18–19
Self-regulation, 33
Self-worth, 61
The Silent Epidemic: Perspectives of High
    School Dropouts, 28
Single parents, 64
Small support, 53–56
Social and emotional learning (SEL), 33
Social media, 44
    interference, 13–14
Society for the Prevention of Teen Suicide, 39
Students
    avoid seeking help from others, 43–48
    engagement resources, 13 (figure)
    find/create connection, 48–50
    mental health needs, 41–43
    peer helpers/mentors, 56–59
    programs and initiatives to stay in school,
        91–93
Students drop out, reasons for
    academic challenges, 11
    bullying and school violence, 14
    chronic absenteeism and truancy, 14
    chronic discipline problem, 12
    cultural disparity, 16
    disconnection, 11–12
    disengagement, 11–12
    extreme poverty, 17
    family mental/physical health issues, 15
    fostering resiliency, 18–19
    lack of grit, 18–19
    language, 16
    peer influence, 15–16
    personal freedom desire, 19–20
    pregnancy, 17–18
    racial, 16
    school resources and supports, lack of, 12
    self-encouraging mindset, 18–19

social media interference, 13–14
student engagement resources, 13 (figure)
substance abuse issues, 16
technology, 13–14
Substance abuse issues, 16
Suicide, 14, 39, 41–42
Suicide Prevention Resource Center, 39

Technology, 13–14
Teen
  efforts, 79–80
  feelings validating, 78

schedule, 78
school and teachers communications, 79
school involvement, 78
Time regulations on technology, 79
Trevor Project, 39
Troublemakers, 12
Truancy, 14

Youth Risk Behavior Surveillance System
  (YRBSS), 41

Zero-tolerance approach, 50

A Sage Company

Helping educators make the greatest impact

CORWIN HAS ONE MISSION: to enhance education through intentional professional learning.

We build long-term relationships with our authors, educators, clients, and associations who partner with us to develop and continuously improve the best evidence-based practices that establish and support lifelong learning.

Solutions YOU WANT | Experts YOU TRUST | Results YOU NEED

INSTITUTES

Corwin Institutes provide regional and virtual events where educators collaborate with peers and learn from industry experts. Prepare to be recharged and motivated!

corwin.com/institutes

ON-SITE PROFESSIONAL LEARNING

Corwin on-site PD is delivered through high-energy keynotes, practical workshops, and custom coaching services designed to support knowledge development and implementation.

www.corwin.com/pd

VIRTUAL PROFESSIONAL LEARNING

Our virtual PD combines live expert facilitation with the flexibility of anytime, anywhere professional learning. See the power of intentionally designed virtual PD.

www.corwin.com/virtualworkshops

CORWIN ONLINE

Online learning designed to engage, inform, challenge, and inspire. Our courses offer practical, classroom-focused instruction that will meet your continuing education needs and enhance your practice.

www.corwinonline.com

PLSN209A8

CORWIN